In this characteristically well-written book, my colleague and friend Mark Sayers delivers an incredibly insightful and prophetic word to a church leadership in that finds itself in deep existential crisis. *A Non-Anxious Presence* is quite possibly the best articulation on the sheer power of liminality to purge, refresh, and renew our way of thinking about leadership that we have at present. It might well be Mark's best book yet.

ALAN HIRSCH, author of numerous award-winning books on missional leadership, organization, and spirituality; founder of Movement Leaders Collective, Forge Mission Training Network, and The 5Q Collective

This is the leadership book I've been waiting for in this season of chaos, disruption, and transition. In *A Non-Anxious Presence*, Mark not only shows us how we got to where we are, he provides a hope-filled path forward. We discover that the wilderness provides an opportunity for renewal, which is exactly what leaders need to lead in these times of constant change.

CHRISTINE CAINE, founder A21 & Propel Women

Mark Sayers has a unique and profound ability to understand culture and, in particular, our cultural moment—how we got here, where we are going, and how Christians might seek to live faithfully amid the tectonic shifts of our age. In *A Non-Anxious Presence*, Sayers casts a vision for pastors and other Christian leaders that allows us to offer hope in a quickly changing and ever-anxious world. Sayers vividly describes the disorienting "gray zone" we now find ourselves in, as well as helpfully interpreting this cultural shift as a "wilderness" of testing in which leaders are called to be refined and purified as we seek the presence of God in our world, our churches, and our lives. Sayers is a faithful, studied, and remarkably insightful guide in this time of upheaval and transition, a time where we find ourselves often befuddled and fearful, a time when God is yet at work redeeming all things.

TISH HARRISON WARREN, author of *Liturgy of the Ordinary* and *Prayer in the Night*

Mark has written another powerful and timely book. Many today are feeling overwhelmed by the chaos and uncertainty our world continually seems to be going through. But becoming a non-anxious presence gives us a compelling vision on how to bring Jesus' peace, leadership, and hope to these deeply troubled times. I am so grateful for a resource like this.

JON TYSON, author of *Intentional Father*; pastor of Church of the City New York

What is the "gray zone"? According to Mark Sayers, it is the time between two eras, the time we now occupy. Everything is in flux. The old hasn't completely passed; the new has yet to arrive. Marked by social uncertainty, this time "between" has led to cultural anxiety. How the church should navigate the gray zone is the subject of *A Non-Anxious Presence*, and this book has come to us at just the right time. Mark's clear thinking, prophetic insight, and practical wisdom are just what we need to lead well in these disorienting times.

BRIAN BRODERSEN, Calvary Chapel Costa Mesa, CA

The message of this book resonates deeply with our experience of the church in Iran. We have had the privilege of learning from and serving with leaders who exhibit "a non-anxious presence." We've seen God use these men and women to build His church amid uncertainty, hostility, and suffering. We urge leaders everywhere to read and embrace the posture this book calls us to.

DAVID (EXECUTIVE DIRECTOR) AND LOUISE YEGHNAZAR, Elam Ministries

This is a message my soul has been craving: prophetic intelligence and fierce hope for those of us seeking to navigate the wreckage of recent events with integrity and a compelling vision. Mark Sayers is a voice I listen to and a leader I deeply respect. His insights are outworked at the coalface of local church in a global city, and they are consistently tempered with prayerful attentiveness to the Lord. For those of us s‌͏ ‍ ‍ ‍ ‍ ‍ ‍ ‍ ‍ ‍ between the Spirit of God and the spirit of the age, Marl message.

PETE GREIG, founder, 24-7 Prayer; Senior Pastor, Emma *Hear God: A Simple Guide for Normal People*

T0026351

It's a new day in today's connected and networked world as leaders who follow Jesus. Mark is a needed and trusted voice in the current cultural context. This is a season for leaders to step up and lead, and this book will serve as a playbook to help you do just that.

BRAD LOMENICK, former president of Catalyst; author, *H3 Leadership* and *The Catalyst Leader*

At one point in *A Non-Anxious Presence* I couldn't stop underlining and marking up the copy with stars and exclamation points. Mark Sayers has given us a leadership book that we badly need for these complicated times. I'm planning to share it with the leaders I serve.

COLLIN HANSEN, vice president of content and editor in chief of The Gospel Coalition and host of the *Gospelbound* podcast

Mark Sayers is like an Old Testament seer. With spiritual eyes he sees the liminal moment we find ourselves in. Times of transition between eras are complex, uncertain, and full of anxiety. Yet Sayers reveals how they are also pregnant with renewal. He calls us to be a non-anxious presence in and for the world, to emulate the patient ferment of the early church, which saw rapid growth in testing times. As a student of different cultures around the world, Mark Sayers has done the unimaginable, capturing the zeitgeist in a way that is as relevant to Asia as it is to the West. In a time of confusion, this book is a spiritual map to chart a way forward into a better tomorrow.

MILES TOULMIN, Vicar of Holy Trinity Bukit Bintang (HTBB), Kuala Lumpur, Malaysia, and Executive Director Alpha Asia-Pacific

Mark Sayers is consistently ten steps ahead of the rest of us, and this book is no exception. I have not read a more insightful analysis of our precise historical moment—its cultural roots, its psychological impact, and its spiritual implications—than I have in these pages. Sayers has gifted us with brilliant insight and understanding that is both honest about our challenges, while also managing to be hearteningly, and realistically, hopeful. I will be recommending this book to every leader I know.

SHARON HODDE MILLER, author of *Free of Me: Why Life Is Better When It's Not about You*

You might just call it deeply insightful and timely. You may as well dare to call it prophetic. Sayers's writing never fails to speak directly in our current situation with much-needed clarity, in-depth analysis, and a bold, gospel-centered perspective. This book is of greatest importance for anybody interested in the future face of church leadership.

JOHANNES HARTL, author; founder, House of Prayer, Augsburg, Germany

In a world where most of us are trying to figure out what on earth is going on, Mark Sayers's sharp, perceptive, and highly clarifying perspective is invaluable. Mark is a voice I listen to at every opportunity, and this book summarizes so much of what every church leader needs to see and to know right now.

CAREY NIEUWHOF, bestselling author, speaker, and host of the *Carey Nieuwhof Leadership Podcast*

The world is changing but we struggle to make sense of it. Mark Sayers argues that we are living in a gray zone, the fading twilight of one era and the early dawn of the next. With his characteristic clarity and insight, he gives us language and imagery for finding our way. This book will make you see the world in a different way; it will make you think and rethink your assumptions and approaches to ministry; but above all, it will lead you to pray—with a hunger and desperation for the Holy Spirit.

GLENN PACKIAM, Associate Senior Pastor, New Life Church; author, *The Resilient Pastor* and *Blessed Broken Given*

Mark Sayers always has a fascinating and insightful commentary on the moment of time we find ourselves in and the kind of leadership that is required.

NICKY GUMBEL, Vicar of HTB and pioneer of Alpha

MARK SAYERS

a non-anxious presence

• • •

How a Changing and Complex
World Will Create a Remnant of
Renewed Christian Leaders

MOODY PUBLISHERS
CHICAGO

Scriptures taken from the Holy Bible, New International Version®, NIV®. Copyright © 1973, 1978, 1984, 2011 by Biblica, Inc.™ Used by permission of Zondervan. All rights reserved worldwide. www.zondervan.com The "NIV" and "New International Version" are trademarks registered in the United States Patent and Trademark Office by Biblica, Inc.™

Scripture quotations marked (NLT) are taken from the Holy Bible, New Living Translation, copyright ©1996, 2004, 2015 by Tyndale House Foundation. Used by permission of Tyndale House Publishers, Carol Stream, Illinois 60188. All rights reserved.

Edited by Connor Sterchi
Interior design: Ragont Design
Cover design: Charles Brock
Cover background texture copyright © 2020 by cluckva / Depositphotos (18857271).
Cover image of gold dust copyright © 2020 by Ukrolenochka / Depositphotos (326055506).
All rights reserved for the images above.
Author photo: Melody Murton

Library of Congress Cataloging-in-Publication Data

Names: Sayers, Mark, author.
Title: A non-anxious presence : how a changing and complex world will
    create a remnant of renewed Christian leaders / Mark Sayers.
Description: Chicago : Moody Publisher, [2022] | Includes bibliographical
    references. | Summary: "For much of recent history individuals and
    institutions could plan, execute, and flourish with their visions of a
    better world. Volatile, complex forces could be addressed and confronted
    with planning and management. But crisis is a great revealer. It knocks
    us off our thrones. It uncovers the weaknesses in our strategies and
    brings to light our myths and idols. Our past strategies run aground,
    smashed by unpredictable and chaotic waves. Yet in the midst of the
    chaos of a crisis comes opportunity. The history of the church tells us
    that crisis always precedes renewal, and the framework of renewal offers
    us new ways forward. A Non-Anxious Presence shows how that renewal
    happens and offers churches and leaders strategic ways to awaken the
    Church and see our culture changed for Christ"-- Provided by publisher.
Identifiers: LCCN 2021060560 (print) | LCCN 2021060561 (ebook) | ISBN
    9780802428578 (paperback) | ISBN 9780802475336 (ebook)
Subjects: LCSH: Church renewal. | Change--Religious aspects--Christianity.
    | Church and the world. | Christian leadership. | BISAC: RELIGION /
    Christian Living / Social Issues | RELIGION / Christian Ministry /
    Pastoral Resources
Classification: LCC BV600.3 .S29 2022 (print) | LCC BV600.3 (ebook) | DDC
    262.001/7--dc23/eng/20220201
LC record available at https://lccn.loc.gov/2021060560
LC ebook record available at https://lccn.loc.gov/2021060561

Originally delivered by fleets of horse-drawn wagons, the affordable paperbacks from D. L. Moody's publishing house resourced the church and served everyday people. Now, after more than 125 years of publishing and ministry, Moody Publishers' mission remains the same—even if our delivery systems have changed a bit. For more information on other books (and resources) created from a biblical perspective, go to www.moodypublishers.com or write to:

Moody Publishers
820 N. LaSalle Boulevard
Chicago, IL 60610

3 5 7 9 10 8 6 4

Printed in the United States of America

contents

Foreword

Anxiety blankets our society and our lives like a thick, wet, bone-chilling fog. It hovers over both individuals and institutions, infusing personal and organizational life with new complexities.

Here's just one example: in late 2019, my research company, Barna, launched a global study of millennials and Gen Zers—more than fifteen thousand surveys conducted from twenty-five countries. We found that one of the *central aspects of the experience of young adults around the world is anxiety*. We even called the first section of our report "Life in the Anxious Age." Despite being more connected than any other generation in history, young adults admitted to struggling with anxiety. This took many forms, from anxiousness about important decisions, feeling pressure to succeed, experiencing uncertainty, loneliness, or mental health issues, and so on.

And that was *before* the coronavirus pandemic.

Of course, anxiety is much more than just a set of angsty feelings or simply the byproduct of worry or unmet expectations. Something fundamental to the human experience is being experimented with, and technological advancements (what I have described as digital Babylon) are the primary laboratory tools.

Anxiety, most broadly understood, also permeates the church and the people who serve as its apostles, prophets, evangelists, pastors, and teachers. Each expression of spiritual leadership faces unique challenges because of the anxious world we inhabit. We are leading and ministering in an anxious age.

And that was *before* the calendar flipped to March of 2020.

Christian leaders find ourselves awash in anxious systems we don't fully understand, blanketed with questions we don't know how to answer.

Yet, Mark's work points the way, like a beacon.

I want to make sure you experience firsthand what Mark has to say, so I won't give away any spoilers, but trust me: I believe this book is going to alter your understanding of the dense problems besetting leaders and what you can do about them. Most books are about the symptoms; Mark's book goes to the roots of the issues.

Every now and then a rare book comes along that defines (ahem) a cultural moment. Mark's book does just that. I think it's a classic and one that I'll be turning to with frequency.

The first two sections of the book help you to orient to the background and nature of the problem; the third section provides practical ways to be formed into a non-anxious leader. I can't wait for you to read and put into practice these hands-on insights. In an expression of 1 Chronicles 12:32—the tribe of Issachar—Mark helps us understand the times and know what to do. (As you might guess, this verse is a favorite of ours here at Barna.)

The ways forward that Mark presents are not mere tips, tricks, and techniques, but faithful patterns of life and perspectives on leadership that could, if applied, anchor us to bedrock—to a God who is called Wonderful, Counselor, the Mighty God, the Everlasting Father, the Prince of Peace.

Finally, perhaps you've read before one of Mark's other excellent books or had the privilege to hear him on a podcast or a stage. I've benefited a great deal from Mark in the past and I think he holds a strikingly insightful and bold role for the Christian community. I am grateful to the Lord for his faithfulness in his calling.

Additionally, I've gotten to know Mark and his wife, Trudi, over many years. They are remarkable and caring people, prayerful friends, co-laborers in Christ, devoted parents, and effective church leaders in Melbourne, Australia. I am grateful for his friendship.

Every now and then a rare leader comes along that defines a *spiritual* moment of opportunity. Mark is that kind of uncommon trailblazer and his gifts are on full display in this book. Thanks to *A Non-Anxious Presence*, I think leaders will be able to see more clearly through the haze of our times.

DAVID KINNAMAN
CEO, Barna Group
Ventura, CA

Introduction

There are times when a whole generation gets caught
to such an extent between two eras, two styles of life,
that nothing comes naturally to it since it has lost all
sense of morality, security and innocence.

HERMANN HESSE, *Steppenwolf*

A thaw set in that night, and all over Vienna the
snow melted, and the ugly ruins came to light again;
steel rods hanging like stalactites, and rusty girders
thrusting like bones through the grey slush.

GRAHAM GREENE, *The Third Man*

You want the soldiers who are dressed in Nazi uniforms to capture the American. That's when the genius of *The Third Man* hits you. In the 1949 film's climax, the Austrian army pursues the corrupted American businessman Harry Lime (played by Orson Welles) through the sewers of Vienna. The scene subverts every World War II movie trope, in which you are hoping that the American will get away from the guys in the German uniforms. It turns the standard moral categories on their head.

The Third Man features the acting prowess of Orson Welles. However, its real star is its location: Vienna in the anxious days following the end of World War II.

The once great capital of the Austro-Hungarian Empire lies in partial ruins—a shadow of the city that only a few decades before had been a magnetic hub of creativity and culture. The city shaped global thought in fields ranging from psychology, economics, philosophy, and the arts. Now Vienna is defeated and humiliated. The empire is not coming back. The global balance of power has shifted. Authority has passed from the Nazis to the Allied occupying forces, who divided the city into different control zones. It was not clear who was in charge. Authority has a habit of shifting around in such places.

The Vienna of *The Third Man* is a gray zone—a transitional space where nothing is black and white. Gray zones are disorientating in-between places, where little seems to make sense. The war has ended, but peace hasn't arrived yet. Elements of its architectural glory exist alongside rubble. Wealth alongside poverty. The dignity of its historic cafe culture continues, alongside the desperation of a growing black-market economy. Morality is malleable. Trust has vanished, replaced by an atmosphere of suspicion. The city is haunted by the past and unable to move into the future. This sense of anxiety is captured in the angular shots and use of shadows, employed by the Australian cinematographer Robert Krasker.

The Third Man's chief protagonist, Holly Martins, stumbles into this confusing gray zone environment in the hopes of building a post-war business career. Unfortunately, his contact in Vienna, Harry Lime, has turned corrupt, showcasing the ways that gray zones change people and relationships. Martins, an American and writer of pulp-western novels, deals in simple stories, with clear lines between who is good and who is bad. Yet, in Vienna, nothing is as it seems. Martin's naïve way of viewing the world runs aground in the complexity of Vienna. The myths of the American frontier don't work in a gray zone. The cavalry never comes.

I won't give away any more spoilers. *The Third Man* is worth watching as a great film. But, more importantly, its portrayal of Vienna as stuck in a gray zone is relevant to us as we live through our own gray zone moment.

A WORLD OF ANXIOUS LEADERS

I thought a lot about *The Third Man* during the pandemic. Unable to travel, I spent a lot of time in Zoom meetings with leaders from across the world. I noticed that despite the different cities, countries, continents, and contexts, a common thread seemed to run through the conversations. As I listened to leaders and pastors, I noticed a particular mood had fallen upon many, a sense that the carpet had been pulled out from under their feet. Despite countless books, articles, documentaries, and TED Talks predicting the impending possibility of a global pandemic, no church leader I spoke to had planned for nor had been prepared by their training for such a possibility. Many wondered what their churches would look like when they regathered. The future no longer looked predictable. Planning became more difficult, pointing toward the possibility of a different future than had been imagined. Some even wondered if their churches would be there when they returned.

Many predicted that the brewing culture wars would subside as the pandemic took hold. Some speculated that a spirit of cooperation would bring nations together, driving a unifying wartime effort to beat back the virus. The opposite happened. Sure, it looked different in different contexts. Yet the effect was the same. The culture wars and social tensions became even rawer, trickling down into congregations, creating new challenges for leaders to navigate.

For several years, I had been helping leaders and pastors understand and lead in the emerging post-Christian society of the West. I wrote, spoke, and podcasted on how we can grow churches of resilience, biblical faithfulness, and discipleship within secular cities. I soon learned that the trends I had outlined were not confined to the West but were reshaping the global church's challenges. Not just in Melbourne, London, or Portland, but also in Lagos, Taipei, and Montevideo. I no longer had to make the argument that a post-Christian moment was coming. Instead, its arrival was making the already difficult task of leadership even more daunting.

A growing sense of anxiety accompanied the rising challenge felt by leaders. The emotional landscape of congregations and Christian organizations was growing more chaotic and unhealthier. Leaders found themselves stuck in the no-man's-land of relational and cultural conflict. Many looked for support but instead found themselves surrounded by anxious friends, spouses, staff, and the marvelous mirages of successful ministry found on social media. Anxiety naturally crept in.

With God, every moment is seeded with the possibility of rebirth. Gray zones offer a blank canvas for God to paint a new story.

Things got worse as heroes of the faith fell. Well-known churches, previously viewed as gold-standard models of ministry, became messes. Great Christian institutions bled legitimacy. Understandably, many Christian leaders began eyeing the exit.

Like Holly Martins in *The Third Man*, we had entered a gray zone. It is a chaotic, confusing, anxious, and complex place filled with change. It is the space between a passing era ending and a new era forming.

How do you lead in a moment like this?

In this book, we will discover how gray zones are seeded with the potential for renewal. Unformed moments and chaotic spaces force us to leave behind the ideas and idols of the passing era. With God, every moment is seeded with the possibility of rebirth. Gray zones offer a blank canvas for God to paint a new story.

It is therefore vital that leaders—not just pastors or leaders of large ministries, but anyone who has a sphere of influence, no matter how large or small—reframe our gray zone moment. We must see it not as a disaster but as an opportunity for rebirth, renewal, and revival. In the Scriptures, the wilderness—that challenging and chaotic place—is transformed into an arena of spiritual growth where leaders encounter the presence of God and become non-anxious presences in an anxious world.

Part 1

The Gray Zone:

In Between Eras

CHAPTER 1

The End of an Era

Indonesia, August 27, 1883

First, the blast sent sound waves that ripped across the face of the earth. Then, a volcanic explosion, ten thousand times more powerful than the atomic bomb, tore apart the Indonesian island of Krakatoa. People heard the sound as far away as Saigon, Bangkok, Manila, and Perth. As the sky turned red and rained rock, churchgoers on nearby islands shuddered, fearing it was the end of days.

The blast killed over thirty-six thousand people, destroying more than three-quarters of the island. The entire planet experienced a raft of environmental effects. Dramatic sunsets and strange phenomena in the sky took place for months. Fire brigades were called as far away as North America. The sky itself looked as if it was on fire.

As news of the explosion ricocheted across the planet, the global public was fascinated. The world was in the grip of the Industrial Revolution, and the rapid growth of technology had elevated belief in human power and potential. For the first time in history, it felt as if nature was tamed. However, the scale of the eruption on Krakatoa awed the world. The modern age again became frightened, reminded of the limits of human ability and the terrifying potency of nature. In an instant, the island of Krakatoa was changed.

For many of us, that is what the world feels like now. The pandemic, cultural change, political polarization, and technological disruption have rapidly altered the world we live in at a breakneck speed. Most understand that the world has changed. However, the sheer rate of change has left many disoriented. We, too, have been left with a sense of the potent chaos in the world. We are not as in control as we thought. We are left with questions of how to lead at such a time when the rules seem to have changed.

REDUCED TO A CHAOTIC FORMLESS STATE

Seven weeks after Krakatoa had burst apart, a Dutch colonial engineer and a small team ventured on the island. Landing, they found the shape and form of the island rearranged. Much of what once was solid had slipped into the sea. Two of its mountain peaks had vanished entirely. Yet the smaller part of the island had grown. The very shape of Krakatoa had been refashioned, birthing a new terrain. Before the eruption, Krakatoa was a thick blanket of trees and plants, which teemed with animals and insects. Yet now, all animal and plant life was vanquished. Its surface turned into a chaotic mess of volcanic rock and ash. The island lay in an in-between state. Not completely obliterated, yet neither able to bear life. This lifeless ground sat in the sea, like the formless land of Genesis 1.

In the biblical account of creation, we encounter unformed earth in its chaotic form. Pregnant with the potential of creation, the Spirit hovered over the waters. The formless earth we encounter in Genesis 1 exists in an in-between state, waiting for birth seeded by the divine hand.

The island of Krakatoa also waited in a formless state. The

island existed in a confusing and jarring in-between form. When reframed, the phase that feels like destruction, mayhem, and death is the moment just before rebirth.

We are moving into our in-between moment, in which the usual rules do not apply. The markers and measurements that we use to find a sense of place and direction do not operate in this phase. This creates anxiety.

Yet we will also discover that in-between moments are filled with potential. They are the moments over which the Spirit of God hovers, waiting to bring new creation. Gray zones are filled with pressure and chaos, yet they are where God does something exceptional inside His people, calling leaders to Himself in a new and more profound way.

First, though, we must orient ourselves at this moment. We need a lay of the land. Once we understand how the world has changed, we can begin to see how God does new and transforming things in transitional moments like this.

WE HAVE MOVED INTO A GRAY ZONE

We are in a time of significant and rapid worldwide change. Political scientist Randall Schweller notes that "the world is undergoing transformation. . . . . a chaotic period where most anything can happen and little can be predicted; where yesterday's rule takers become tomorrow's rule makers, but no one follows rules anymore; where competing global visions collide with each other; where remnants of the past, present, and future coexist simultaneously."[1] The lightning change was happening in politics, technology, culture, and the global order, hinting at a new and different future.

These changes only seemed to accelerate with the arrival of

the COVID-19 virus. "This virus, like many before it, is just such a history-accelerating crisis,"[2] note journalists John Micklethwait and Adrian Woolridge, illuminating the way that pandemics launch us into new epochs. Yet as the third decade of the twenty-first century begins, we find ourselves in an unnerving transitory state—the gray zone.

> **KEY IDEA:** *We have not entered a new era; instead, we have entered an in-between phase, a gray zone.*

WE ARE LIVING IN A GRAY ZONE

Confusion is the dominant sense we experience during transitional moments of rapid change. Therefore, it is vital to understand where we are and what is going on.

We need a new interpretive framework to understand the abnormal conditions that are emerging in the world. The framework I would like to offer to help us understand this moment is simple. The world is moving into a transitional phase—a gray zone.

A gray zone is confusing and contradictory, filled with change and conflict. Everything seems to be up in the air.

I have borrowed the term *gray zone* from the study of twenty-first-century warfare. Traditionally, there were clear definitions of what war was, when it started and ended. It was clear who was fighting and what rules of combat were. However, it is becoming less apparent in the twenty-first century when war has begun and when it ends.

When mysterious soldiers in unmarked green uniforms turned up in the Ukrainian region of Crimea in 2014, no one knew if this was a local insurgency, an invasion from Russia, or something new. It was the start of a new conflict, yet no one could tell exactly when the war began. This shows how the boundaries between war and peace are blurring. Military strategists now differentiate between kinetic war—essentially shooting and blowing up the enemy—and other forms of war such as cyber, information, legal, criminal, psychological, and economic.

Understanding this background helps us understand why gray zones are confusing places. The term *gray zone* has a broader application than just as a military term. Many Christian leaders—who have been formed by procedure, clear boundaries, and sharp definitions—find this moment challenging to comprehend and operate within.

GRAY ZONES EXIST IN THE OVERLAP OF TWO ERAS

Historians arrange passages of time into eras. Eras traditionally are shaped around the rule of an empire or ruling class, which establishes an overarching big story or narrative. Big stories are created and communicated primarily by those in power to justify their rule. Eras also contain a defined set of rules and promoted patterns of life. History shows us that an era tends to be dominated by influential individuals who shape its thinking, key events that determine its direction, movements that embody its longings, and artists who capture its mood.

> **KEY IDEA:** *Gray zones exist in the overlap of two eras. They contain the influence of both the passing and forming era; this makes gray zones confusing and contradictory.*

However, there are moments when ages overlap and eras mingle in a hybrid transitional moment. Thus, gray zones contain the influence of more than one era. Historian Peter Gay captures this in describing the interwar years of his childhood in Germany, which was marked by a mood that "was both old and new. The striking mixture of cynicism and confidence, the search for novelty and for roots."[3] For people living through the years in between the world wars, it seemed to many like a new beginning. To others, it felt like the end of an era. Thus, gray zones are bridges in between eras.

So how do we know when we are in a gray zone or living through an era? Let's dig deeper.

GRAY ZONES CONTAIN AN INTENSIFICATION
OF THE PASSING ERA

Gray zones exist in the overlap between the passing era and the era to come. One can be fooled that the old era is still dominant. Often as eras pass, their traits intensify. We have seen this dynamic at play during the pandemic. The effect of lockdowns created a radical break with routine. No longer could we look away from the realities of the era we had been living in. As the British novelist James Meeks reflected on the lockdowns, "When you aren't going anywhere, the danger is that you might start seeing the way things are going."[4]

Without the daily distractions and routine of our lives, the concerning trajectory of the era we lived in became clearer. The crises under the surface became impossible to ignore.

As Dani Rodrik writes, "The crisis seems to have thrown the dominant characteristics of each country's politics into sharper relief. Countries have in effect become exaggerated versions of themselves." The pandemic was serving to "intensify and entrench already-existing trends."[5] In nations across the world, a range of social issues that had been simmering under the surface burst forth—bringing forward a raft of issues such as racism, religious tensions, sexism, and the environment. The problems of the era were intensifying at the precise moment that the era was passing.

GRAY ZONES CONTAIN THE TRAITS OF THE COMING ERA

At the same time, however, we could also see a new world being born. For most of the last decade, a series of impending shifts have been visible on the horizon—trends that will have a far-reaching impact on our world. The globe, in the words of Richard Robb, James Manyika, and Jonathan Woetzel, stands

> poised at a set of historical, technological, economic, political, and social inflection points. The transformation we're living through has sometimes been likened to the Industrial Revolution. In fact, the Industrial Revolution pales in comparison to today's convulsions, because the shifts today are happening much faster and on a much bigger scale. Because they are so interlinked—urbanization and consumption, technology and competition, ageing and labor—and because they amplify one

another, the changes are harder to anticipate and more powerful in their impact. And they challenge our imaginations as much as they do our competencies and skills.[6]

One of the impacts of the global pandemic was to accelerate us toward that horizon and those inflection points. The pandemic didn't change the world. It was a signal of the change already happening in the world. British historian Adam Tooze described the pandemic as "a way station on an ascending curve of radical change,"[7] noting that "for better or worse there is no escaping the fact that 'big things' are going to happen. The continuation of the status quo is the one option we do not have."[8] The world was already a change-rich environment; the pandemic was a harbinger that the continual and accelerating change was here to stay.

Indian novelist Arundhati Roy observed that COVID-19, like all pandemics, operated as a bridge between eras, a portal between the world we have lived in and a new world yet to be imagined.[9] As a result, our movement became more local. Yet, at the same time, we became more digital. With the rise of new technologies from rapidly developed vaccines to the mainstream adoption of disruptive innovations such as cryptocurrencies and the normalization of remote work, the future seemed much closer.

We follow an unchanging God, who is advancing His kingdom in this gray zone moment.

A futuristic mood emerged during the pandemic. Cryptocurrencies became mainstream. Viral videos showcased rapid advancements in robotics. The Pentagon began reporting on encounters with UFOs. Economist Tyler Cowen remarked, "I have been reading science fiction for half a century, having spent my childhood consuming it in various forms. Now, for the first time in my life, I feel like I am living in a science fiction serial."[10] It's clear that a new era is being born. Its contours are unclear, yet its influence is still palpable. This is what it feels like to live in a gray zone.

> **KEY IDEA:** *The gray zone will be the context in which you will live and lead. We must understand it and learn to flourish within it.*

We may not know without hindsight when the gray zone will end, yet it is the environment in which we are called to lead. To live out the kingdom of God. For those who have found themselves overrun by the sheer pace of change over the last five years, who anxiously try to find their bearings in this time—you are not alone. Gray zones are challenging places that operate under different rules. However, we follow an unchanging God, who is advancing His kingdom in this gray zone moment.

As we will discover next, gray zones are precisely the kinds of places that God seeds with renewal and rebirth.

RECAP: THREE KEY TAKEAWAYS

- We have not entered a new era; instead, we have entered an in-between phase, a gray zone.

- Gray zones exist in the overlap of two eras. They contain the influence of both the passing and forming era; this makes gray zones confusing and contradictory.

- The gray zone will be the context in which you will live and lead. We must understand it and learn to flourish within it.

CHAPTER 2

Rebirth

Three years after the initial visit to Krakatoa, another expedition landed upon the island. Instead of burnt, barren ground, the landing party discovered that life had again taken hold in this most unlikely of places. Mosses, algae, flowering plants, and even species of fern flourished. How had these plants managed to grow in such a barren and dead environment? Tiny seeds carried by the wind or birds had triggered a miraculous renewal of life upon the devastated island. Seeds beget seeds. Seeds turn into fruit. Fruit turns into seeds, and multiplication occurs.

A year later, another expedition arriving on the island discovered that "there had been . . . rampant growth. There were now dense fields of grasses, so tall that a man could hide himself,"[1] writes Simon Winchester. Destruction had paradoxically led to a rebirth of life. Today the island is the repository of an ecosystem of thousands of plants and dense forests. It is home to hundreds of animal species.

What looked like destruction was the phase before germination. The devastation created a blank page upon which a new story could be told.

What looked like destruction was the phase before germination. The devastation created a blank page upon which a new story could be told. The gray zone became the seedbed of renewal. Krakatoa reminds us that what may look like decline, loss, or even obliteration can be revival's launching pad. For such renewal to occur, all it takes is a single seed.

THE WORLD IS SEEDED WITH RENEWAL

The metaphor of seeds helps us understand how God transports His dream of redemption for the world. His Word creates new life, renewing and reviving. At the fall, Adam and Eve rejected God's good order in the world. Instead, they chose a new path of sin. As a result, death and destruction rushed into the world, warping and wounding the good creation that God had wrought from chaos. Instead of tearing up His plans and annihilating His handiwork, God chose the path of redemption. God initiated a project of renewal that would undo the pattern of death and chaos in the world.

To renew is to make new, to bring back to life. We see this most clearly as Jesus—God in human form—took death and sin upon Himself on a Roman cross. For three days, the Son of Man, like a seed, lay in the cold ground. Yet on the third day, Jesus rose. The power of resurrection was let loose in the world. A new spiritual era was born. Salvation was now available to all who fell at the feet of the risen King. Those who decided to follow Him would become more like Him. Renewal has been released in the world, and the powers of darkness cannot stop it. Even in our gray zone moment, God is moving history toward His ends. For those with eyes to see, the seeds of renewal are everywhere.

> **KEY IDEA:** *When viewed through a biblical lens, gray zones are moments that often precede renewal and rebirth.*

Seeds of Renewal in the Church

There are seeds of renewal in the church. There is a hunger for renewal, revival, and awakening brewing among God's people. For a period, it was possible to bury one's head in the sand and ignore the challenges of secularism and post-Christianity. Now, however, the decline and stagnation are stark. It is undeniable that the surrounding culture can warp churches and believers. We feel the gap between the vision of the church we encounter in Scripture and the reality on the ground. This gives rise to a deep desire for God's church to be refreshed, empowered, and renewed.

There is a longing among God's people to see His church live out its potential. This hunger for renewal is happening across denominations. This longing is global. Across the world, from Scandinavia to South America, there are thousands who see the culture changing rapidly and who pine to see the presence of God fall in new ways to revive His church.

Seeds of Renewal in Us

Accompanying the hunger for God to revive His church, many believers today also hunger for personal renewal. They long for a deeper walk with God. They desire a more transformative faith. There is a deep sense that millions have fallen into the contemporary pattern of life, one of continual consumption, ever-present anxiety, and self-focus—an unsustainable pattern. Many are realizing that what they long for can only be satisfied by the eternal God. Be assured that seeds are being laid for a great renewal of our personal faith.

Seeds of Renewal in Society

There is also a growing international hunger for a renewal of society. Over the last decade, we have seen protest movements across the world call for reformations of society. Many issues have come to the fore, such as economic inequality, corruption, environmentalism, racism, sexism, and farmers' rights. These issues have sparked massive movements in nations across the world, both online and in the streets. Emerging technologies are making it easier for such movements to grow and organize. They shine a brighter light on injustices and corruption. It is now harder for governments, corporations, and institutions to maintain their public face without scrutiny. This dynamic is leading to a global crystallization of discontent. Hence, a growing and now ever-present hunger for a resounding renewal of society.

> *God distributes the seeds of renewal via leaders who carry the seed of renewal.*

KEY IDEA: *God has seeded the world with renewal. God uses leaders to seed His plans in the world.*

GRAY ZONES ARE SEEDBEDS

God has seeded gray zones with the potential for renewal. Life was returned to Krakatoa in the form of seeds carried to Krakatoa via ocean currents, gusts of wind, and birds. In the same way, God distributes the seeds of renewal via leaders who carry the seed of renewal. Leaders who, by stepping into the process of renewal, find themselves renewed. A renewed leader is a leader who then leads others into renewal. These leaders become carriers of the seed of renewal, embodying the next season God is birthing among His people.

Yet often, such leaders are unaware of how God works, unattuned to His processes. As a result, many such leaders lie dormant, hidden in the gray zone, waiting to be activated.

Yes, there are times when it appears as if the darkness is winning. When the direction of culture, the circumstances of our lives, the poverty of spiritual life among God's people seems tilted toward difficulty, decline, and even death rather than renewal. This is particularly true during our gray zone moment. The church seems divided, the culture unraveling, and the world reeling toward chaos. Yet, at moments like ours, we must remember that God has seeded the world with His dream of renewal. The pattern of Scripture is that this dream is planted within leaders.

KEY IDEA: *God seeds leaders with His dream of renewal.*

We see this pattern throughout Scripture and church history. For even in the seemingly darkest and most confusing times, God still brings forth a new cohort of leaders—ordinary people with an extraordinary role to play as carriers of His seed of renewal. Through surrendering to God's will, they discover and then advance His pattern of renewal in the world. Yet, for these seeds to be activated, leaders must step into a process of growth. As we will discover, the life cycle of seeds is a reeducation into how the world works.

RECAP: THREE KEY TAKEAWAYS

- When viewed through a biblical lens, gray zones often precede renewal and rebirth.

- God has seeded the world with renewal. God uses leaders to seed His plans in the world.

- God seeds leaders with His dream of renewal.

CHAPTER 3

The Victorian Internet

The lush growth, spreading across the gray zone of Krakatoa, was not the only new life that had appeared in the nineteenth century, mysteriously carried by the sea. Just as Krakatoa had sent shockwaves across the world, a new technology was also reshaping the late nineteenth century.

The laying of undersea telegraph cables had transformed how news was communicated around the globe. Historian Ben Wilson recounts that the invention of the telegraph created a global network of communication that "profoundly affected the way people related to each other and experienced the world. From a plantation worker in Berar to a reader of a newspaper in Dresden, people were bound to each other by new, invisible and often unsettling networks of information exchange."[1] The creation of this mechanical World Wide Web birthed the international news media as we understand it today. The news spread with speed and infectiousness, akin to how pandemics had previously gone viral across the planet.

The eruption of Krakatoa became the world's first mass media event. News of the explosion shot across the globe via the telegraph network, capturing the world's attention. "It took an event like Krakatoa's eruption—which astonished and mystified an entire educated world—to underline the real revolution that this new technology was visiting upon the planet."[2] At first, this information revolution was heralded with the kind of almost religious optimism that accompanies the advent of new technologies in the modern age. The ability to quickly pass information around the world, to read about news from around the globe, was predicted to unify nations and cultures. The techno-optimists proclaimed that it could potentially end wars and usher in a new golden epoch for humanity.

This information revolution, however, also delivered an unexpected fruit.

Historian Tom Standage has labeled the telegraph the Victorian Internet, noting that "the information supplied by the telegraph was like a drug to businessmen, who swiftly became addicted." But, like all drugs, there was a powerful side effect—anxiety. One New York businessman of the time warily observed that "there are doubts whether the telegraph has been so good a friend to the merchant as many have supposed." Instead, users of this new global information network were "kept in continual excitement, without time for quiet and rest."[3] The ability to be continually connected empowered those who relied upon the telegraph, enabling them to ship goods across the world or trade stocks in foreign markets. However, it also spread anxiety across the globe.

RESTRUCTURING THE WORLD

As we will discover in this chapter, just as the modern world brings technological breakthroughs, advancements in science, and greater individual freedoms, it also creates anxiety. Anxiety is viewed as an individual ailment, and indeed many experience it as such. However, as we will learn, there is a structural element to anxiety.

We are living through a profound structural change in our world. Moments of structural change create a sense of cultural anxiety, which every leader must understand.

> **KEY IDEA:** *The structure of our contemporary world creates an anxious social atmosphere that can paralyze leaders.*

Let's continue to see how the restructuring of the world in the nineteenth century created anxiety—learning the parallels to our day.

AN ANXIOUS GLOBAL VILLAGE

Simon Winchester writes that "with the explosion of Krakatoa came a phenomenon that in time would come to be seen as more profound. It would not be stretching a point to suggest that the Global Village was essentially born with the worldwide apprehension of, and fascination with, the events in Java that began in the summer of 1883."[4] The phrase "global village" was coined by the Christian Canadian media theorist Marshall McLuhan. For McLuhan, the global village is not a warm, reassuring image of a world brought together by technology but rather a place of terror and anxiety—less a small, quiet village, and more the world as a whole in all its noisiness and complexity brought close. These new connective technologies created a gray zone in which everything overlapped. The reality of constant connection ate away at the markers that formerly rooted people in place, giving them an identity. Place and people defined our identity, yet new technologies such as smartphones have connected us to those far away, rendering where we are from as less essential to our sense of self. "When ordinary people do not know who they are, they get anxious,"[5] cautioned McLuhan.

As the world in the nineteenth century took its first technological steps to become a global village, anxiety birthed a whole raft of new and previously never before encountered illnesses. The afflicted were the citizens of the burgeoning cities of the industrial revolution. Women complained of nervous disorders, living with a lingering sense of never feeling at ease. Other women found themselves swamped with negative feelings, experiencing what the medical practitioners of the day called "hysteria." Men suffered from what was named "brain fevers," "brainstorms," and "nervous exhaustions." Experts labeled the phenomenon *neurasthenia*.[6] American writer William James used the phrase "Americanitis,"[7] a term that captured how the new American lifestyle made individuals anxious and exhausted. Anxiety became normative, and people found themselves overcome with a constant doubt they had done something wrong.

Strangely, this was occurring as much of the West was enjoying a period of rapid economic growth and global stability. This period punctuated by the shattering of Krakatoa would be known by the French label the *Belle Époque*, which translates into English as the beautiful era. The Austrian writer Stefan Zweig called it the "Golden Age of Security."[8] While it may not have been a golden period for the poor and many working people, a middle class was born. Yet it was those middle and upper classes enjoying this unprecedented period of stability, comfort, and predictability that were most ravaged by the gnawing anxiety. It was those who had gained the freedoms of the emerging modern world, such as the rising middle classes, women, and the newly minted rich. Newfound freedoms brought newfound fears.

The culture went searching for a solution. In response rose a variety of proposed answers, from the rise of psychoanalysis with pioneers such as Sigmund Freud to the advent of the positive thinking self-help movement. In its infancy, Coca-Cola was sold as a remedy for anxiety disorders. Rests, retreats, vegetarianism, and vacations rushed into vogue among those suffering from suffocating anxiety. Yet little seemed to work.

STUCK IN ANXIETY

Evan Hopkins had a strong faith and felt called to his ministry. Yet like many Christians of the late nineteenth century, he faced a crisis.[9] Hopkins was a South American engineer of Welsh descent. He had spent part of his life in Australia before migrating to his ancestral home in the UK, where he felt the call into ministry.

As we learned, like so many living in the rapid cultural change of the late nineteenth century, he found himself confronted by a sticky anxious morass. What should have been his greatest joy—living for Jesus—felt like a struggle. An anxious lethargy had overtaken his life. Discipleship was reduced to an ongoing plodding forward, perpetually hoping for a breakthrough but never getting there.

Just as there appeared to be a link between cultural anxiety and a period of comfortability, the Belle Époque birthed worry. The same dynamic also seemed to blunt the mission of the church. Martyn Lloyd-Jones, looking back, warned that we should "never forget the pride and arrogance of the Church in the nineteenth century. Behold her sitting back in self-satisfaction, enjoying her so-called cultured sermons and learned ministry. . . . Observe the prosperous Victorian comfortably enjoying his worship. How constantly he denied the Spirit of the New Testament!"[10] Wealth, stability, and comfort had appeared to blunt the mission of the church. Comfortable times create comfortable Christians.

The number of men and women of God overcome by emotion and exhaustion at the end of the nineteenth century is remarkable. John Pollock writes that believers in the late nineteenth century were "slowly suffocating in an atmosphere of introspection and gloom. Fervent Christians groaned, and gloried, in unceasing inner conflict."[11] They kept their faith, the church continued, and hope for renewal remained.

Yet a kind of quiet resignation became normal. Many accepted the belief that the life of faith was a dull, exhausting struggle. At the very moment that the world had been linked by a new technological network, presenting a unique opportunity to spread the good news of Jesus around the globe, anxiety had seemingly blunted the activation of the seeds of renewal. Revival had retreated underground to lie dormant.

KEY IDEA: *Christians can become mired in sticky anxiety, infected by the broader cultural mood of the day.*

STUCK IN THE PAST

Christians of the late nineteenth century stood on the shoulders of previous generations of revival and renewal. They found themselves struck down with the same ailments as the culture. The culture-shaking, church-reviving awakenings of the past had seemingly faded. Viral outpourings of faith had washed over the world for over a century. Such an outpouring came during the Second Great Awakening of 1858–1860. Yet as church historian David Bebbington records, "Thereafter, however, there was no similar international awakenings during the nineteenth century."[12] There were minor outbreaks of renewal and revival, but they were localized. In other places, they became routine. Revivals were reduced to rote annual fixtures in the calendar, devoid of power and presence. Instead of the overflowing waves of revival that had previously swept the world like the shockwaves of Krakatoa, a worrisome introspection became normative as believers became more focused on their inner worlds than on a world to be reached with the gospel.

ANXIOUS PRESENCES

In our day, anxiety has become one of the significant ailments of our world. Yet it is also a signal, an alarm that something is desperately wrong in our world. We must differentiate between the individual mental health challenge of anxiety, which a minority of individuals in every culture experience, and the systemic anxiety that our contemporary culture's structures create.

> *A worrisome introspection became normative as believers became more focused on their inner worlds than on a world to be reached with the gospel.*

The late Edwin Friedman, rabbi and family therapist, argued that anxiety became a dominant factor in contemporary culture. Friedman's central argument was that modern American society was awash in worry. He warned that "the anxiety is so deep within the emotional processes of our nation that it is almost as though neurosis has become nationalized."[13] Sketching out how anxiety affects us first at a corporate level, Friedman noted that "anxiety escalates as society is overwhelmed by the quantity and speed of change."[14]

In our gray zone moment, institutions have lost legitimacy in the eyes of much of the public, coming under significant pressure and pushback. Friedman discovered that one of the social functions that institutions play is to absorb anxiety. Humans create institutions to pass on wisdom, to collectively conquer challenges, to centralize critical knowledge. It is an accepted fact among political scientists that well-functioning and healthy institutions are the bedrock of peaceful and prosperous societies. Just think of the way that a well-functioning medical system can allay our fears over a health concern. However, with the devaluing and disappearance of institutions, individuals were left to absorb the culture's anxiety. Anxiety then becomes a systemic phenomenon. By classifying anxiety as a personal issue rather than a systemic issue, we place an enormous burden on the individual, who then must modify their personal lives to alleviate the suffering that anxiety brings. Instead, Friedman taught leaders that they must understand that anxiety resides in networks of human relationships.

SEEDING A MOMENT

For Evan Hopkins and his peers, a new kind of renewal was about to move. It was post-denominational. It was breaking out in small meetings, retreats, and conventions in the countryside. God was about the business of refreshing His people. The Spirit was blessing His children.

For Evan Hopkins, his moment from anxiety to activation occurred at a small Christian meeting in Mayfair, London. Hopkins was struck, along with others in the room, by the truth found in

2 Corinthians 9:8 that "God is able to bless you abundantly, so that in all things at all times, having all that you need, you will abound in every good work." So pivotal was this moment that he called it his May Day experience.[15]

The reality is that God wishes to bless His children. The work is God's. There was a hope for a different kind of faith beyond just the faith of struggling through defeat. This truth broke out from these small meetings across the world. God outpoured on a whole new generation of believers the vision that God wishes to bless His children with deep, joyous faith and a peace that transcends human understanding.

At the precise moment in which it seemed like God had stopped moving and His followers became stuck in a quicksand of anxiety, the Holy Spirit was seeding the landscape and planting in hearts dreams of renewal and revival—personal refreshments that would grow into movements and transform into mission. The moves of personal renewal that occurred in gatherings, retreats, and conferences during the late nineteenth and early twentieth century would lay the foundations for the modern missionary movement. This renewal would eventually spread out across the globe to the four corners of the earth. The anxious were transformed, becoming courageous frontline servants of a new global move of the gospel. The late nineteenth century appeared to be a fallow period. Yet there were seeds of revival, dormant in the ground.

KEY IDEA: *When viewed through kingdom lenses, comfortable, prosperous, and stable times do not always equate to good soil. Comfort can insulate us from renewal.*

Seeds contain the imprint of the trees that they will eventually become. However, for seeds to grow, they must sprout past what is called the coat. That is the protective outer casing of the seed. At first the coat protects, then it restricts. A seed that is unable to move past this barrier is unable to grow. It remains paralyzed, stuck in the ground. The coat, created to protect the seed initially, can prevent it from developing into what it was designed to be. As we will discover, the structures that we build to soothe our anxiety, to protect us, can prevent the activation of the seeds that God has placed within us.

Strongholds are protective structures created by humans to insulate us from external threats and to reduce our anxiety. The Scriptures focus on the strongholds built by humans, noting how they can become an alternative to God.

Next, we will turn to the greatest stronghold humans have ever created—the American century.

RECAP: THREE KEY TAKEAWAYS

- The structure of our contemporary world creates an anxious social atmosphere, which can paralyze leaders.

- Christians can become mired in sticky anxiety, infected by the broader cultural mood of the day.

- When viewed through kingdom lenses, comfortable, prosperous, and stable times do not always equate to good soil. Comfort can insulate us from renewal.

Part 2

An Anxious World:

From Stronghold
to Network

CHAPTER 4

Life and Leadership on Secular Autopilot

How do you remake the world when it seems like it is falling apart? How do you keep the growing threat of chaos at bay? With World War II raging worldwide, a small group of around fifteen men, all members of a think tank known as the Council on Foreign Relations, met in the safety and luxury of their New York townhouse located just off Central Park, asking these very questions. As one group member wrote, "I suppose it comes hard to realize that the foundations of the order of things as you know it may have ceased to exist."[1] The men anxiously began to set out their plans. Their task? To remake the world. How? By creating a zone of control—a protective area that would stretch across a swathe of the globe, keep the chaos out, and bring peace and prosperity.

By the midpoint of the twentieth century, the global information network of the telegraph had not fulfilled the promises of its most optimistic champions. The idea that connection and communication could stop war and bring the world together now seemed laughable. The Belle Époque had collapsed, and the chaos had returned.

It began with the unthinkable shock of World War I, which

killed and maimed millions, shattered the European empires, and permanently changed the global order. The war was not even over before the world cascaded into the Spanish flu pandemic's masks, lockdowns, and catastrophic death toll. After the pandemic came a burst of pleasure-seeking energy. Traditional conventions were thrown out the window. Gender norms were blurred in fashion, art, and cinema. New social movements sprung up everywhere. The established order was placed under continual pressure.

New media and entertainment reshaped popular culture. Disruptive technologies sped up the world. Everything seemed to be moving too fast, especially the stock market, which collapsed into a devastating global financial depression. This collapse was a boon to the political fringe. Soon the streets would see battles between the far left and the far right. The politics of race returned with force. The growing chaos birthed both revolutions and totalitarian regimes.

A haunting fear that democracy was soon bound for the graveyard lingered. An unstable international order, with competing nation-states and no defined center of power, would quickly fall into a second devastating global war. An era was passing. The world had moved into a gray zone. Finally, however, a new era would arise—an era that would both shape our world and our leadership imagination.

LEADERSHIP FOUNDATIONS

Our culture gives us an archetype of what a good leader looks like. As an Australian, I have culturally programmed into me a uniquely Australian archetype of what it is to lead. It's likely based on my national values of mateship and egalitarianism. In Australian culture, leaders mustn't take themselves too seriously. Nor can they forget that they are an ordinary person. This means that authority in

Australia is held uncomfortably and is constantly defused, both by followers and leaders, through self-effacing humor. Whatever your national background, how we think about and understand leadership rests on a foundation of cultural assumptions.

The times in which we live also mold our vision of leadership. The modern world that has spread across the world through globalization carries its cultural assumptions. It operates as a kind of meta-culture, existing alongside our national cultures. This means that the modern world shapes our understanding of what it is to lead. Moreover, as we will learn in this chapter, the contemporary world emerged from the American century. This means that there will be an overlap between American cultural assumptions of leadership and the leadership imagination we find in the modern world for American readers. But first, we must examine how the modern world has shaped our understanding of leadership for all of us.

> **KEY IDEA:** *Our understanding of leadership rests on a set of cultural assumptions. These cultural assumptions are shifting as the world moves into a gray zone phase.*

When culture shifts, when the foundations of the modern world change, it will reshape our leadership imagination. Just think, thirty years ago, to lead and have influence, to have your voice and ideas heard, you needed to work your way up to the top of an influential Christian organization. Or you had to become the senior pastor of a big or significant church. Leadership impact and influence were built over decades. Today, however, Christian social media influencers have far more sway and influence, shaping the views and thoughts of the Christian world; the footprint of their impact is more significant than those with large churches or at the top of Christian institutions and organizations.

This shift is having a massive impact on the church, transforming our view of leadership both in the eyes of those who lead but also in the expectations of those who are led. This shift, however, is simply reflecting a cultural change. Power in our globalized world is shifting. This results from structural changes around technology, which is reshaping what it is to lead. Nevertheless, national culture is still vitally important and continues to frame our leadership.

To lead in our gray zone moment, we must understand how our understanding of leadership is shifting. To do that, we need to explore the making of our modern world and how it has shaped our leadership imagination. In order to see the shift, we must first connect with where it all started. This will help us grasp the gravity of the transformation currently underway in the world, aiding us to better understand how leadership is morphing.

Let's return to Manhattan during the dark days of World War II, as a small group of men designed and dreamed up the world that we take for granted.

TO REMAKE THE WORLD

The group, cloistered away, sketching out their plans for a new world, was known as the War and Peace Studies group, a subcommittee of the Council on Foreign Relations, a powerful and influential think tank. Represented were economists, Wall Street bankers, media magnates, Ivy League academics, military chiefs, and the future director of the CIA. Their brief? To plan for a new post-war global order, which would, in the words of one group member, "think of world-organization in a fresh way."[2] They would remake the structure of the world.

The United States had imagined itself as a natural stronghold, protected by two oceans. This gave it both physical and psychological distance from the dysfunctions and drama of the "old world." However, as the globe became interconnected, the seas no longer created a defensive stronghold. Now, the waves of chaos seemed to be lapping at the United States.

INVENTING THE FREE WORLD

The crux of the subcommittee's solution to the problem of growing global chaos is captured in this summation by Stephen Wertheim: "The superior coercive power of the United States is required to underwrite a decent world order. . . .to prevent the international realm from descending into chaos,"[3] to move the world out of the chaotic and dangerous gray zone moment that had emerged in the 1920s and '30s. A plan was established to create what was called "the Grand Area"—a vast economic, cultural, and political stronghold, which would maintain order and keep out the chaos.

The group realized that much of the American public, and indeed the public of other nations that this new configuration of the world would dominate, would need convincing as to why US dominance was a good thing. So the "Grand Area" moniker would be refreshed with the more marketable label of the "Free World." Yet behind these labels was something as ancient as the Scriptures. The "Free World" was what the Scriptures call a stronghold, which is a metaphor and image used throughout the Bible, particularly in its poetry, describing fortresses, high places, and refuges, where safety and security is found.

We will explore in-depth in the next chapter the biblical

Any attempt to arrange the world as a functioning, peaceful place where humans can operate without God is a secular project.

metaphor of the stronghold. But first, we must note that any plan to refashion the globe is ultimately a spiritual endeavor. The modern world, which sprung out of the world-making project of the Council on Foreign Relations, set the foundation for a secular world in which humans don't need God. Historian Ayesha Ramachandran observes that "few ideas have become so thoroughly associated with the emergence of modernity as that of a globalized, interconnected, secular world. The phrase 'modern world' has in fact become a shorthand for a global environment characterized by scientific rationalism, large-scale economic networks, and agnostic skepticism."[4] To put this simply, any attempt to arrange the world as a functioning, peaceful place where humans can operate without God is a secular project.

The modern world grew out of the enlightenment principle, espoused by Thomas Paine, that humanity had it in their power to begin the world again. This is an act of world-making—the act of turning a wilderness of complexity and injustice back into an Eden. Walter Lippmann, the columnist and member of the War and Peace Studies subcommittee, recorded that the group's focus was "not the prevention of war, but a satisfactory organization of mankind."[5] This was more than another global project or an attempt to facilitate peace. This was an alternate gospel—the creation of a stronghold apart from God.

The stronghold and structure of the modern world have shaped how you both view and experience your life. The stronghold of the contemporary world can turn even the religious into practical atheists. How? By furnishing the possibility of operating on a kind of secular autopilot, we can move through our lives without thought or need for God, since the modern world will deliver all of our needs. We assume that the item we purchase online will arrive on our doorstep. We take for granted the logistics, human energy, and natural resources that are consumed in order to furnish our contemporary lifestyles—a vast array of hidden servants making our lives easier, all while providing for our comfort and needs, contributing to a sense that history will inevitably move toward a better future.

> **KEY IDEA:** *The modern world promises progress and perfection without God. Leaders formed by the contemporary world can therefore presume that dependency on God is optional.*

The structures of the modern world implicitly promise that we can operate as leaders, even as Christian leaders, without thought or need for God. Instead of our foundation being in Christ and His kingdom's way of influence, we rest on the cultural foundation set by the modern world of what it is to lead. We measure leadership with earthly definitions of success and power. A secular autopilot version of Christian leadership takes hold, where we lead like practical atheists, with God as an afterthought.

However, this very structure, which has furnished the secular possibility of living without God, is shifting.

WE PRESUME ONGOING STABILITY IN THE ENVIRONMENT

A Christian leader can move into a kind of secular autopilot because we assume that the basic structure and stability of the modern world will naturally continue. While we recognize that some change may occur, like evolving cultural norms or technological innovation, our general assumption is that the environment in which we operate will essentially remain stable and ordered. We presume that the basic infrastructure we rely on, supply chains, transport routes, and institutions, will remain operational.

As we will discover, this assumption leads to a false security in which we can presume that dependence on God is optional. Yet the environment is changing. As a result, the structures of the stronghold are shifting.

SOFTWARE, STRONGHOLDS, AND STRUCTURES

We must examine the strongholds and the structures in which we live. We overlook their power because we see ideas rather than structures as the primary change agents within history, viewing our culture as a battleground of ideas. Ideas do indeed shape our world and do change our culture.

When we simply see the world of ideas, we presume that we can change the world by spreading our preferred ideas. We try to intellectually defeat the ideas that we see as false or dangerous. We work to keep bad ideas out of the organizations, institutions, and individuals we lead.

We presume that change occurs through top-down dissemination of ideas distributed by powerful and charismatic elites and influencers. This assumption leads us to believe that if we are to change society for the better, we need to get our people at the top of the ladder to promote our ideas downwards.

KEY IDEA: *More than a change in our thinking or simply the introduction of new ideas, we are living through a profound and far-reaching change to the very structure of our world. This structural change has enormous implications for how we lead and live.*

When it comes to change and influence, we can tend to think of ideas like software. However, there are times when a new idea comes and changes our culture in the way that a new software update may improve the performance of your computer. For example, during the process of writing this book, my laptop has automatically downloaded new software. To be honest, I have barely noticed this happening; it mainly occurred in the background. Yet if I were to swap my Mac for a PC during the writing of this book, that would be an entirely different scenario. It wouldn't be an issue of new software, but rather, new hardware altogether. The very structures would be changed.

Philosopher Bertrand Russell noted that it was not the intellectuals with their ideas who had the most influence, but rather, the real power lay with the technicians—those who build and fashion the very structures of society. My argument is that we are living through more than a software update or the downloading of new ideas. Instead, we are living through a hardware change. The internet as we have known it is morphing into a metaverse. The energy sources that have powered the last century of growth are being replaced, creating new challenges. The vision of globalization that the global order has been built around is being rethought. Our model of economics is entering uncharted waters. The geopolitical order is shifting toward the Indo-Pacific. New technology is changing politics. The gray zone moment we are in is one in which the very structure of society is shifting.

Robust societal structures spread more than simply control; they also spread culture. They shape the thoughts, feelings, desires, and attitudes of those living in that time. They form the places we look to for solace, strength, hope, comfort. We will discover that they also shape our leadership imagination, creating models in our minds of what leaders look like, what it means to lead, and how influence is used. When the very structures of society change, everything changes.

As we will discover in the next chapter, the structures and strongholds in which we live create buffers for our anxiety. Their legitimacy is derived from making us feel safe and implicitly promising to give us an unfettered environment to pursue our best lives. Yet they constrict and warp our models of leadership. When they shift, they change what leadership looks like.

RECAP: THREE KEY TAKEAWAYS

- Our understanding of leadership rests on a set of cultural assumptions. These cultural assumptions are shifting as the world moves into a gray zone phase.

- More than a change in our thinking or simply the introduction of new ideas, we are living through a profound and far-reaching change to the very structure of our world. This structural change has enormous implications for how we lead and live.

- The modern world promises progress and perfection without God. Leaders formed by the contemporary world can therefore presume that dependence on God is optional.

CHAPTER 5

The American Century

When anxious and concerned about our safety, stability, and security, we create strongholds. In the ancient world, nomads would band together in tribal groups, gaining protection in numbers. As agriculture brought greater stability and security, settlements eventually grew into cities. Cities enabled the storing of seeds and crops—their walls insurance against the unpredictability of nature.

The concentration of people in cities enabled the concentration of knowledge and birthed schools and guilds, which facilitated the development of expertise and technical advancements. The wealth that cities could generate through trade and taxation could raise armies and fund armaments. A city was a zone that humans could control, its walls designed to keep out chaos and evil. The city expanded the possibilities of human power. Cities would band together to form confederations, kingdoms, states, and nations. Each grouping was incrementally increasing the power of humans.

The stronghold is a biblical metaphor. A stronghold is a fortified area with strengthened walls. It can be reinforced by the natural defensive properties of geography, such as hills and high places, that keep the enemy and the evil out. Psalm 18:45 speaks of people trembling with fear as they leave the safety of their strongholds.

KEY IDEA: *Strongholds form when humans seek out or build a protective structure to find security, safety, and prosperity in a threatening, chaotic, and unpredictable environment.*

We can trace back to Eden our desire to seek strongholds outside the will of God. The sin of Adam and Eve in the garden was to reject God's way, choosing instead to build their own order. One thing that differentiates humans from God is power. God possesses more power than a human. The serpent's temptation was for Adam and Eve to grow into gods by gaining power apart from God. It was, of course, an impossible project. Divine power only flows from God. Yet this temptation remains, hovering before all people, to grow in power apart from God. Thus the wilderness, the in-between places of danger, creates a fear in us beyond the immediate physical fear of being harmed.

The ancient Israelites and their pagan neighbors agreed that any god worth their salt could battle against the chaos of nature and win. A human exposed to the chaos and danger of nature is reminded that they are not a god. Our vulnerability and mortality is exposed. Our lack of control and powerlessness is laid bare. Outside of the stronghold, anxiety becomes our constant companion.

THE IN-BETWEEN SPACES

Ancient travelers moving from the stronghold of one city to another found themselves particularly vulnerable. They anxiously moved through a gray zone, the unfamiliar and treacherous in-between. After killing his brother Abel, Cain walked in fear. Genesis 4:14 tells us that despite God's reassurance over his safety, Cain wandered restlessly in his vulnerability and mortality. He was separated from God's presence and east of Eden. Cain builds a city, a stronghold of protection for his family. Its walls are a replacement for the protection and presence of God.

The architectural plans for strongholds are first drafted in the anxious human heart.

The ancient traveler lived in constant fear, worriedly wandering like Cain east of Eden. After their journey through the badlands and open spaces, the sight of a stronghold appearing in the distance would fill the traveler with hope, extinguishing the anxiety that plagued their journey through the in-between.

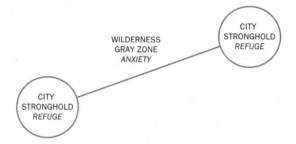

Safe in the walls of the stronghold, the human finds respite from their fears. This illuminates an essential truth for us. When we are anxious, we seek out strongholds. When we cannot find a stronghold, we build one. We seek to centralize control and power in a stronghold. The architectural plans for strongholds are first drafted in the anxious human heart. Strongholds are humanity's oldest antidote to anxiety.

Once a stronghold is established, it will become attractive

to those who find themselves in uncertain, in-between spaces. A stronghold becomes magnetic, a vision of hope and home for the worried and lost. Strongholds that appear adequate and sturdy will become beacons to those who find themselves filled with the anxiety of living in the in-between spaces. They grow in size and power, taking on lives of their own.

In our gray zone moment, in which anxiety rises, it is worth pausing and reflecting on the strongholds that we may look to find solace. As leaders lose legitimacy both in the broader culture and even in the church, where will we look? What stronghold are we drawn to outside of the will of God? As society secularizes, the church appears to drift into a religionless future. What strongholds within our culture do we seek out? It is at these moments of vulnerability and discouragement that the strongholds of our day are most seductive. These are important questions, for as we will discover, as people are drawn to strongholds, their power increases.

THE CENTRALIZATION OF CONTROL AND POWER

Humans build strongholds as a means of finding protection from other humans. Strongholds form in competitive environments as rivals and other groupings set up their own strongholds. In the Bible, we see this anxious balance of power as different tribes, nations, and peoples compete for power. Once the walls of a stronghold are built, it is an admission that the people within its walls are in competition with the forces outside.

A pattern observable throughout history is that once a stronghold begins to grow in power, it begins to seek dominance among, and eventually over, the competing strongholds that surround it. This path to dominance usually occurs through technological innovation, military superiority, economic power, and access to crucial resources. These advantages lead to the stronghold gaining dominance. An example of this is how a capital city becomes dominant in a nation. It draws talent, trade, and tourism to itself.

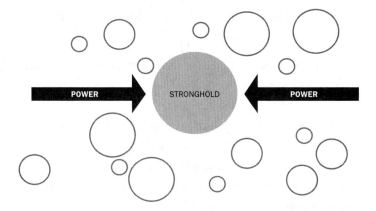

The stronghold becomes the central hub within the system of strongholds. Domination then leads to a centralization of power. Having gained dominance, the stronghold—be it a state, kingdom, brand, or organization—will consolidate power and control through growing and evolving several elements, such as:

- The **formation of a hierarchy**. The arrangement of power within the stronghold, with clear leadership at the top whose primary job is to maintain the dominance of the group.

- A **defining narrative** that both explains and justifies the centralization of power. This defining story will also build the foundation of exceptionalism—how the stronghold is superior to its rivals. Accompanying practices and symbols form. These symbols and stories take on a kind of sacred meaning.

- **Command of communication** enables the dominance of the defining narrative and the stronghold's way of life over potential dissenting voices.

- **A way of life.** Universally encouraged values, protocols, practices, and patterns that align with the continuation of the stronghold's power.

- **Institutions** that formalize the values, protocols, practices, and patterns of the stronghold.

These elements transform a stronghold from simply protective walls into something denser. Purpose is found in a thick web of social and symbolic meaning. As a result, the stronghold grows in its power and complexity, becoming an environment that powerfully shapes our thinking and understanding of the world.

THE SEED OF PRIDE

As our strongholds grow and develop, something dangerous can also grow within them. Psalm 52:7 warns of "the man who did not make God his stronghold but trusted in his great wealth and grew strong by destroying others!" Strongholds enabled people to farm in safety and to store seeds and grain. In a broken world, strongholds can protect and preserve us. However, the Scriptures warn us that they also can be fertile ground for another more insidious seed—the seed of pride. With the seed of pride taking root, the stronghold becomes an earthly alternative to dwelling in the presence of God.

Strongholds, built for refuge, have a habit of transforming into seedbeds of pride.

Strongholds, built for refuge, have a habit of transforming into seedbeds of pride. The stronghold may also project power beyond its boundaries to secure resources while seeking ways to expand its capacity. The most powerful and tangible example of this dynamic throughout history is an empire, where one nation dominates and rules other nations and peoples. The dominant stronghold shapes the culture, social system, thought, and practice of other less powerful groups.

KEY IDEA: *An era is a period in which a stronghold in the form of a state, kingdom, corporation, or organization maintains dominance over a system, projecting its power and control outward.*

An era is a period in which a stronghold is dominant over a system of other weaker strongholds. Thus, we speak of the Victorian era as a way of speaking not only of the reign of Queen Victoria but also the order that was projected into the world during her reign.

GLOBAL SUPREMACY

The Council on Foreign Relations members understood these dynamics as they planned for a new global order during World War II. Their goal was to make the United States the dominant power within the world system. Their means of achieving this would be through creating a global economy, benefiting the United States. A growing economy would ensure a powerful military. A powerful military would ensure that the international connections and trade routes could be secured and essential resources accessed.

This strategic arrangement established a new era in the world. The media magnate Henry Luce, a member of the War and Peace

Studies group, captured the moment's mood, proclaiming the birth of the American century. As World War II ended and peace broke out, a new era had begun.

As the United States became the dominant power in the world, it birthed many smaller yet still powerful strongholds within itself that would project their power into the world—Hollywood, Wall Street, NASA, Madison Avenue, Silicon Valley. It spawned large corporations such as Ford and Exxon Mobile, the NBA, Ivy League colleges, and the CIA. Each spread its influence and control throughout the United States and the world.

The American era of domination seemed complete by the start of the nineties. The Cold War had ended with the fall of the Berlin Wall, leaving the United States the lone standing superpower presiding over a new order of globalization. This global order promised a new golden age, a global civilization, built on the trade of consumer goods and open cultural exchange.

The American era shaped more than just American minds; it also transformed the mental landscape of vast parts of the planet. The American stronghold now stretched across the globe.

KEY IDEA: *The American century is the unexamined cultural foundation upon which much of our leadership frameworks, strategic assumptions, and measurements of success rest.*

CRACKS IN THE CONTROL ZONE

However, the dream of the American century was interrupted by a series of shocks, beginning with the attacks of 9/11. Next came the global financial crisis, which led to the Arab Spring, and a new kind of global protest movement of dissent against established mainstream powers. This reaction against the elite class of the globalized world reached the West in the rise of the antiestablishment and populist political backlash, epitomized by Brexit and the election of Donald Trump. The downside of social media and the internet became more apparent. Fake news, misinformation, and trolling became planetary problems. Power was diffusing and decentralizing, moving away from the central strongholds that had shaped culture.

These unexpected outcomes pointed to a different kind of future than was imagined. Heavily invested in the vision of a peacefully progressing globalization, many among the elites and the general populace chose to interpret these disruptions as interruptions rather than the pains of a passing era or omens of the era to come. Technological innovations such as ride-sharing, streaming services, and e-commerce seemed to confirm that a smoother way of life was emerging. These developments fueled the sense that the culture-wide disruptions were mere hiccups. However, as disruption continued unabated, a deep sense of worry began to take hold.

At the start of the third decade of the twenty-first century, the same global network designed to facilitate a comfortable new world through speed and ease of movement became the accelerant of the spread of a virus—tiny in size, but global in impact. No longer could the individual ignore the hyperconnected dynamic we now lived in. What happened in a city such as Wuhan could fundamentally alter the lives of millions of individualists.

The intensification of individualism that had marked the start of the twenty-first century was defined by a naïve belief that while the world may change, our ability to continue pursuing our personal desires, plans, and patterns would not be affected. Yet an event on the other side of the world, which started small, could have significant effects on our lives. We discovered that we were not as free and autonomous as the American century led us to believe.

That all this could stop in a matter of weeks seemed unimaginable, yet weirdly it wasn't. We had seen this movie before. Hollywood had filled our screens and thus minds with apocalyptic images of fallen, empty cities. As Russian historian Alexei Yurchak recounted the experience of living through the collapse of the Soviet Union, "Although the system's collapse had been unimaginable before it began, it appeared unsurprising when it happened."[1] We truly were entering into the gray zone.

When a stronghold is unable to continue to operate as a buffer for our anxiety, its legitimacy comes into question. American historian Barbara Tuchman noted that orders break down and historical change occurs "when the gap between the ideal and real becomes too wide." What happens then? "The system breaks down."[2] Once the legitimacy of a stronghold is questioned, it no longer absorbs our anxiety. Instead, it becomes the source of our anxiety. We shift from the ambient anxiety that is present in times of affluence, peace, and stability to the sharper, more irrational anxiety that comes when the whole system seems to be breaking down.

As we move into the transitory and unfamiliar space of the gray zone, leadership models and frameworks of the previous era will begin to come under tremendous pressure. We need a different way forward. Before we get there and learn a different way of leading, we first need to examine what kind of world we are now entering.

RECAP: THREE KEY TAKEAWAYS

- Strongholds form when humans seek out or build a protective structure to find security, safety, and prosperity in a threatening, chaotic, and unpredictable environment.

- An era is a period in which a stronghold in the form of a state, kingdom, corporation, or organization maintains dominance over a system, projecting its power and control outward.

- The American century is the unexamined cultural foundation upon which much of our leadership frameworks, strategic assumptions, and measurements of success rest.

CHAPTER 6

Birth of a Networked Age

I am looking at a photo from *Life* magazine in 1959 entitled "A Valuable Bunch of Brains." The image features members of the influential RAND Corporation think tank plotting to change the world. The setting is the mid-century modern Laurel Canyon home of Albert and Roberta Wohlstetter. Tribal and abstract art fills the room. It could be a scene from the TV series *Mad Men*, as the group lounges on the modernist furniture, engulfed in a haze of pipe smoke. You can imagine a Dave Brubeck jazz LP playing in the background. This small group of diverse and brilliant minds would nestle themselves in the very center of power at the height of the American century. Their dreams and schemes would alter the shape of the American century.

A NEW WAY OF SEEING THE WORLD

It was the zenith of the Industrial Age. Automobiles were pouring off the assembly lines of Detroit, a testament to how Henry Ford's invention of the assembly line had changed the world. Mass production was birthing a mass culture—a society of consumption, suburban tract housing, and mass media. As Stefan K. Link records,

"The power of the assembly line thus extended far beyond the factory, giving rise to an entire system of social and cultural imperatives,"[1] creating a world that worshiped at the shrine of efficiency and productivity. This was more than just a means of making cars; it was a remaking of society. Creating "a distinctively American modernity that is said to have spread across the world in the twentieth century."[2] However, at this moment of triumph, anxiety had set in.

There was a challenger to the United States' crown as ruler of the industrial era. The launch of *Sputnik*, the world's first satellite into space, had propelled the Soviet Union ahead in the race to become the preeminent global power. As *Sputnik* passed over the United States at night, it brought a palpable sense of national insecurity. Future president Lyndon B. Johnson would recall, "Now, somehow, in some new way, the sky seemed almost alien. I also remember the profound shock of realizing that it might be possible for another nation to achieve technological superiority over this great country of ours."[3] Anxiety set in. So the best and the brightest put their minds to the task of envisioning new ways to ensure that the stronghold remained impenetrable.

New thinking was indeed happening at the Wohlstetters' home. The circle of RAND Corporation intellectuals was rethinking how the United States could maintain its supremacy in its struggle with communism. The group's research in a diverse field of studies, from science and mathematics to anthropology, psychology, social studies, and even modern art led them to a new way of viewing the world. The "RANDites turned the concept of human knowledge on its head," argues journalist Alex Abella; they had "posited a new view of human existence."[4] At the new frontier of the modern age, these innovators needed a new model of understanding how power worked. This search leads them to a new way of seeing the world, which would shape our contemporary society. Their key finding, their new model of understanding reality was this: the world was a system—a complex, connected network.

This new way of seeing the world leads to further questions about power, strategy, and influence. If the world was a vast, complicated, and interconnected system, how does one control this system? How do you bring order into a network, halting its descent into potential chaos?

If the world was a network, this changed the rules of the game.

The answers given and the solutions implemented by small but influential groups such as the RAND Corporation would lead to the world we live in. Data, technology, and the social sciences would play a central role in this new networked world. The seeds of a new form of globalization driven by consumerism and the establishment of a vast digital network would be laid in the mid-century by small groups of innovators like the RAND Corporation.

KEY IDEA: *The world is a system—a complex, connected network.*

These solutions were designed to give the United States a new platform to control the world system. Yet these innovations would drive a significant decentralization, which would spread power away from the center and outward throughout the network—laying the foundations for our gray zone moment.

The political scientist Yuval Levin states that this decentralization would drive a cultural diffusion that "didn't begin all at once: the transition lasted for decades and went through various phases."[5] This is not the place to trace this whole history. The critical point to grasp is that the first years of the American century were the height

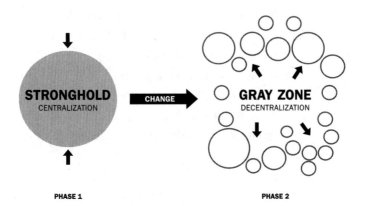

PHASE 1   PHASE 2

of the centralized institutions. Life orbited around big industries, mass media, large government bureaucracies, churches, community organizations, and unions. Power moved toward the center. However, as the decentralizing impulse grew within society, these strongholds began to leak power, influence, and credibility. Power moved outward.

As the decades passed, the impulses of both the political left and the right worked in tandem to diffuse the center's power. The left moved away from its traditional focus on workers' rights. Fighting instead for greater individual freedom from conventions and taboos, they put their shoulder to the deconstruction of cultural norms. The right also sought freedom, but in the economic realm, pushing back on what they saw as the centralizing influence of government.

Despite the calls for greater collectivism and community spirit on the left, and the right's desire to return to the traditional values of family, faith, and national service, the fruit of their twin efforts produced the same result—decentralization, a shift from central institutions to a network of loosely connected individuals. These processes progressed over the decades at a robust pace. However, in recent years, decentralization has accelerated.

Two key elements have rapidly accelerated this decentralization.

THE DRIVERS OF OUR DECENTRALIZATION

Globalization

The centralized American world created two factors that drive its decentralization and loss of power. The first factor was baked into the American century—globalization. The economic order created by the United States imagined a world of free trade in which goods, services, and people would freely circulate the world to benefit the United States. Globalization expands the number of connections in the global network. The more connections established by the central power, the more likely the possibility that power may shift from the center out into the network.

Globalization offered other nations the chance to compete with and even potentially displace the United States from its central position. The larger and more connected the network, the harder it is to control. This is indeed what is happening now. The world is shifting from the era of an American-led globalization to an increasingly global globalization.

Mass migration, tourism, trade, and global popular culture have all accelerated during the era of globalization, creating a more interconnected world. In addition, technological advancements such as jet travel and the global supply chain have made the world a much smaller place. However, one technology is rapidly increasing our connectivity beyond anything seen before in history.

The Internet

The Industrial Age created the computer. The digital age began when computers were connected to each other in a network, creating the internet. The arrival of smartphones facilitated continual connection to the digital network, expanding its reach into our daily lives. The internet overcame the tyranny of distance, enabling connection anywhere on the planet. Once you are continuously connected to the world, you see the world differently. Norwegian anthropologist Thomas Hylland Eriksen observes that globalization increases our awareness of our interconnectivity.[6] We are more attuned to what is happening outside of the physical environment in which we live. We are everywhere and nowhere all at once.

However, the internet not only allowed us to create more connections across the world's landmass. Instead, the dense web of online connections it made turned into a kind of new territory—cyberspace. Former US diplomat Henry Kissinger, who understands shifts in the global order, reflects that "cyberspace challenges all historical experience," creating a novel situation where "a laptop can produce global consequences"[7] and where small players are empowered with the ability to influence and disrupt the global network.

Globalization and the internet are the two primary factors driving our networked reality. Two networked environments—the physical world and digital cyberspace—are increasingly connected in a symbiotic relationship. With the growth of the "internet of things," our physical devices are plugged into the internet, such as cars, refrigerators, and smartwatches. Our online and offline worlds will, according to Adam Segal, "merge to such a degree that we will no longer always be able to differentiate them."[8] This will only intensify our connectivity and the scope of the digital network. The internet of things and other emerging technologies such as crypto-currencies, virtual reality, and 3D printing will only further accelerate our decentralization.

DECENTRALIZATION AND GRAY ZONES

As we have learned, the motivation to build strongholds is driven by anxiety. In all their forms, the walls of strongholds are designed to keep the bad out. However, as we will learn, networks have a way of going around stronghold walls. This means that in our networked world, anxiety returns.

Our gray zone will not be a fleeting moment but rather an indefinite period of ongoing disruption and instability as the patterns that have defined the world for the last half-century are radically reshaped. To grapple with the immense changes occurring within our society, we need to understand why this change is happening.

Decentralization occurs when power and influence are dispersed throughout a network. Decentralization is ultimately about control. This shift is birthing a networked world in which power is diffused in multiple locations, spread through a network rather than centrally held. This shift is as immense as other crucial turning points in history, such as the establishment of the Silk Road, the advent of the printing press, or the Industrial Revolution. Perhaps more so, for it contains the power to change global society at every level.

To flourish, lead, and live in the twenty-first century, we need an understanding and sense of how the decentralizing impulse of networks operate, what Joshua Cooper Ramo calls "The Seventh Sense." "The Seventh Sense, in short, is the ability to look at any object and see the way in which it is changed by connection."[9] The networked nature of our world is the shift behind the shift. It is creating the crisis behind the crises. It is the pattern of our age, which replaces the previous era's order, which then creates a gray zone dynamic. We have learned how strongholds develop and centralize power—projecting power and dominance and beginning an era. Now let's understand how this decentralizing shift from stronghold to network occurs.

KEY IDEA: *The fundamental structure in the world is no longer central institutions but networks.*

HOW AN ERA ENDS

Eras can come to an end when a centralized power begins to lose its dominance and its ability to project power. This can be caused by an economic collapse, defeat in war, internal political division and civil war, hubris and moral decline, or the devastation wrought by a pandemic or natural disaster. Or, as Paul Kennedy observed, when the cost of projecting power financially exhausts the centralized power.[10]

With an era coming to an end, the centralized power can no longer maintain dominance over the playing field in which they operate. A new contender enters the fray—a rising competitor who possesses the potential to overtake the declining power. The increasing power may have a breakthrough technology, a growing economy, a powerful military. Or as Chinese political scientist Yan Xuetong argues, the rising power may benefit from better leadership than the dominant power.[11] Some historians posit that such a dynamic almost always leads to a war between declining and rising powers.[12] The old era fades. The rising power becomes dominant. By centralizing power and projecting an order, they initiate a new era.

NETWORK DYNAMICS DRIVE DECENTRALIZATION

This pattern has been repeated throughout history. Yet it is rarely a clean and linear process. This is where the concept of gray zone clarifies the kind of transitional moments we are living through. We need to take a step back and understand how power forms in human society. We need to imagine the world as a kind of giant system filled with connections. Historian Peter Frankopan writes, "Just as anatomy explains how the body functions, understanding these connections allows us to understand how the world works."[13] The world is a network of relationships.

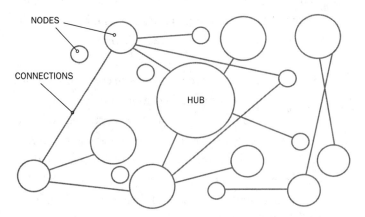

Understanding how networks work is vital. A network is made up of four key elements.

- **Nodes**—The individual elements of the network could be a person, a computer, or a salmon within the ecosystem of a river.

- **Connections**—These are the relationships that link nodes in the network. A connection could be a friendship, a trade route across an ocean, or a computer cable.

- **Hubs**—These are highly connected nodes in the network, through which multiple connections in the network pass. A hub could be a port city like Venice during the medieval period, a social media platform like Facbook, or a university like Oxford.

- **Protocols**—The rules and values upon which the network operates. Liberal democracy is a protocol upon which many nations operate. The World Wide Web works as computers communicate with Internet Protocol (IP) addresses. One of the protocols of international relations is that negotiations between nations are often conducted in French.[14]

In a network, connections count. We need connections to give us access to social support, vital information, and the ability to buy and trade essential goods and services. To be an isolated node with no connections is a dangerous place. This means connections create power in a network. Hubs—the places in a network that multiple connections pass through—inevitably become powerful. This could be a city like London—a financial, diplomatic, governmental, and cultural hub. Or it could be an internet platform like Twitter or

Facebook where millions meet to connect digitally. Or as Malcolm Gladwell has shown, it can also be a highly socially networked individual such as Paul Revere, who was able to single-handedly garner a military response to the British attack upon Lexington, due to the dense relational connections he had built up with connected individuals and influential institutions.[15]

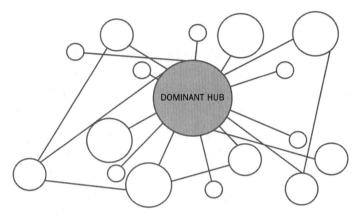

When a nation-state, organization, or institution becomes a powerful hub, it begins to centralize the power of the network toward itself. Nodes become dependent on the hub as the essential place of connection within the network. The flat nature of the network is transformed into a more vertical hierarchy as the hub gains prominence within the network. The dominant hub can control the protocols of the network, thus creating an order that ensures that the nodes of the network must follow its values—something we currently see as Big Tech battles to establish its set protocols over what kind of speech is allowed on their platforms. The hub has gained dominance. We then are back to where we started, the era of centralized dominant power, a stronghold projecting its order.

As a power fades and a rising power emerges, an in-between

process must occur. This in-between process is the gray zone, which begins as the dominant hub loses the ability to project its power, thus loosening its control of the network. This reverses the direction of power. Power is diffused, spreading out through the web.

THE DIFFUSION OF POWER

Power and influence are never stationary within a network. An example of this was the news report I just watched, which reported on millennials leaving Paris to move to smaller cities and rural areas. This trend accelerated during the pandemic, not just in Paris but in major cities across the world—a reversal of a trend in which the power and influence of cities as significant hubs within the network drew people to them, a dynamic that has been operational since the Industrial Revolution. Intriguingly this trend had begun before the pandemic in China. As the nation built a highly effective and widespread high-speed rail network, remote work has made it possible to mix the benefits of a country lifestyle with a good job. This is an example of how influence and power can move away from hubs out into the network.

> **KEY IDEA:** *In a network, power is fluid. It moves around the network, creating new sources of power and undermining old power centers.*

Once power shifts away from hubs, the network returns to a flatter pattern. Just think of video production. Only a few decades ago, the ability to produce high-quality video was only held by those with large budgets such as television networks and film studios. This gave them tremendous power and influence. Now, however, anyone with a smartphone can produce high-definition video, enabling YouTubers and influencers to gain significant cultural traction at a fraction of the price, as power has drained away from mass media. With power spread through the network, new connections are enabled, which don't pass through the once-dominant hub. As a result, new hubs begin to develop. Coalitions of smaller nodes and hubs form, gaining power through their combined connectivity and building influence in the network through pursuing joint objectives.

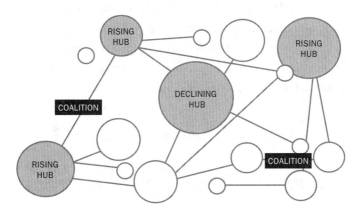

There is no one dominant hub within the network in this development phase but rather multiple zones of control. This leads to several shifts. First, numerous hubs and coalitions vie for power. The once-dominant central hub can no longer maintain control over communications, and a vast array of communications floods the system. Story wars (battles over which narrative will define reality) replace the singular defining narrative in which a dizzying array of narratives battle for dominance. People worry less about the singular dominant communication of the government and start worrying about disinformation and dangerous conflicting stories.

This places new pressures on organizations, leaders, and churches in our gray zone moment. Danish social scientist Bjorn Thomassen notes that in-between times present "a peculiar kind of unsettling situation in which nothing really matters, in which hierarchies and standing norms disappear, in which sacred symbols are mocked at and ridiculed, in which authority in any form is questioned, taken apart and subverted."[16] That which was accepted is now continually challenged.

Centralization is replaced by decentralization. Multiple influences and orders now vie to exist in the network, causing power to swirl fluidly. Control gives way to competition. The stability and clarity of a defined era are replaced by the instability and undefined nature of a gray zone. The once-dominant stronghold may still be powerful; however, the structural reality has changed.

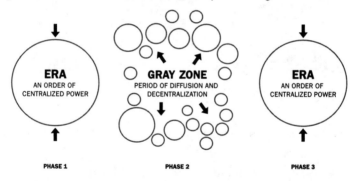

This is a pattern repeated throughout history. According to historian Niall Ferguson, a networked era "followed the introduction of the printing press to Europe in the late fifteenth century and lasted until the end of the eighteenth century."[17] The period saw the dominant hubs of the church and the feudal system radically disrupted. Power decentralized due to the technological innovation of the printing press and the information revolution it unleashed.

"With the advent of printing, books became more widely available and now lay well within the reach of an economically empowered middle class. . . . Laypeople were beginning to think for themselves and no longer regarded themselves as cravenly subservient to the clergy in matters of Christian education,"[18] writes Alister McGrath. This innovation decentralized and distributed knowledge. Cultural, social, religious, and political life was radically changed. We are again entering such a period, and its effect potentially will be as significant.

Futurist John Robb observes, "We are now living in a world where networks are at the center of our existence."[19] The network is now the primary structure forming the world, our culture, and our personal lives. So decentralization is here to stay.

The significant effects of decentralization can already be seen in the growing tribal dynamic at work within the world.

GRAY ZONES DRIVE TRIBALISM

Before strongholds, in dangerous and conflicted environments, humans banded together in tribes. Tribes were mobile, tightly connected, and united in a joint mission to survive without protective walls of a stronghold. They found meaning in the protective stories, shared interests, and tight relational ties of the tribe. In our gray zone moment, as strongholds lose their integrity, so do our concepts of identity.

In our gray zone moment, as strongholds lose their integrity, so do our concepts of identity.

With no agreed-upon defining story or shared values, identity becomes something the participant in the networked society must search for themselves. Many search for meaning and identity in regionalism, nationalism, political parties, single-issue causes, or self-expression. The Spanish sociologist Manuel Castells notes that in our global network, "The search for identity, collective or individual, ascribed or constructed, becomes the fundamental source of social meaning." Humans have always found meaning in identity. However, a networked world lunges us into a new social situation in which "identity is becoming the main, and sometimes the only, source of meaning."[20] Decentralization leads to atomization, in which the individual is cut loose from traditional sources of relationship and identity, finding meaning only in the "atom" of self. The atomization created by decentralization creates a new tribalization. Contemporary life is lived in the gray zone between this drive to individualism and tribalism.

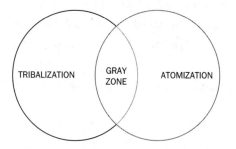

British political commentator David Goodhart argues that globalization has created two types of people—the anywheres and the somewheres.[21] The anywheres enjoy the benefits of the new networked world. They move comfortably through cyberspace and around the physical world. Their identity is the identity of the global network. The ability to move around networks freely is the new marker of power. Power is the ability to live in multiple places at once. To have the power to pick up and leave. The sense of meaning traditionally found in "place" is replaced with the freedom found in the app.

The network does not define the somewheres. They find meaning in place. Instead, they feel they are the losers of the shift to a networked world. "Globalization is increasingly seen to work for the few, not the many,"[22] comments political scientist Stephen D. King. "Somewheres" have seen the global network send their jobs overseas, ruining the social fabric of their town or region. They feel aggrieved that their way of life is mocked by "anywhere" elites. "Somewheres" feel that they were loyal and productive members of

Decentralization leads to atomization, in which the individual is cut loose from traditional sources of relationship and identity, finding meaning only in the "atom" of self.

the passing era, finding meaning in its defining narrative, many having served in the armed forces to defend this era's values. Yet now they feel disoriented and discarded by the new global network. Those left behind, who feel that the stronghold has let them down, look to the tribe.

This feeling of alienation from the networked world is recognized and mobilized globally by both left and right populist political movements. "Behind every one of these movements is the idea of restoring order in a chaotic world by reestablishing borders. They represent the ultimate reaction to a boundary-less world made up of global networks and the flow of communication,"[23] notes Jeremy Rifkin. Ironically, this protest against our networked age has been aided by the digital network itself. For discontents, social media offers a chance to find a lever of protest, to forge new online tribes of the disaffected.

In this digitally driven tribal pushback, the network is used to attack the network. Politics in many countries has shifted from trying to win office by forming a middle consensus platform that appeals to the most voters. Now the game is about creating an insurgent platform that appeals to a tribal dynamic. This dynamic drives forward the pattern of decentralization.

THE END OF THE AMERICAN CENTURY

For the last half-century, an American-led global order has dominated the world economically, militarily, politically, and culturally. The United States has been the dominant hub of the worldwide network it built. However, as Fareed Zakaria argues, while the United States remains the world's most powerful political and military state, "In all other dimensions—industrial, financial, educational, social, cultural—the distribution of power is shifting, moving away from American dominance. . . . we are moving into a post-American world."[24] Even as American power fades and other powers rise, its influence upon the world is still active in the gray zone. The domestic instability of the United States, caused by the end of the American century, is still exported globally, adding to the volatility of the world.

China will likely surpass the United States in terms of gross domestic product in the next decade. It will create a new hub within the global system as it builds its global network in the Belt and Road

Initiative. This does not necessarily mean that the next era will be a Chinese-dominated international order. Instead, as political scientist Charles Kupchan writes, "The next world will have no center of gravity. It will be no one's world,"[25] with multiple and shifting centers of power, competing political and technological models, and rival concepts of morality and justice.

The future is a decentralized world.

Now we have gained a big picture understanding of how decentralization is changing the world. Next, we will focus on understanding how decentralization is changing ministry and leadership on the ground. Finally, we will discover what it is to lead in a gray zone and how we can flourish in such places with God.

RECAP: THREE KEY TAKEAWAYS

- The world is a system—a complex, connected network.

- The fundamental structure in the world is no longer central institutions but networks.

- In a network, power is fluid. It moves around the network, creating new sources of power, and undermining old power centers.

Part 3

Leading in the Gray Zone:

The Ways of the Wilderness

CHAPTER 7

A Non-Anxious Presence in an Anxious Age

You may not have understood the dynamic of decentralization before reading this book; however, I am sure that you have felt the impact of this shift. This chapter will dig into how this shift has brought the cultural battles occurring within the broader world into many of our churches and Christian organizations. In addition, this change is remolding leadership. Leadership was once seen as the art of building consensus. However, now it can feel like the act of desperately avoiding conflict—a change that is creating anxiety in many leaders. We will then examine Edwin Friedman's solution to this problem, a posture for leaders to adopt, the non-anxious presence.

FROM THE GOOD KARMA NETWORK TO NETWORKED CONFLICT

The Good Karma Network began to build social cohesion and community spirit in the Melbourne neighborhood of Brunswick. The network quickly grew in popularity as neighbors found a forum to pass on produce from their home gardens—a place to locate tools to share and used goods to swap. The success of the Good Karma Network made it a showcase of the potential that digital networks could bring to a physical community.

However, this good news story turned bad. By 2021, open culture war had engulfed the network. Its moderators stood accused of "toxic positivity." Accusational posters featuring their faces were plastered around the very neighborhoods they had tried to improve. The charge was that the group's narrow focus—only communicating positive news—was implicitly racist. In their final message before shutting down their page, the moderators wrote, "We have now reached a point where we as admins are not safe, in public or online. Our names are being shared online with no regard for our safety or wellbeing."[1] The mood of communal connectivity, which had blossomed in 2016, had a short few years later descended into full-blown conflict.

In this chapter, we will discover how a more connected world becomes a more conflicted world—exploring how the world is moving away from unified globalization toward a more fragmented reality in which tribalism replaces consensus. Institutions and leaders find themselves engulfed in new dynamics of conflict.

KEY IDEA: *A more connected world is a more conflicted and therefore anxious world.*

THERE ARE NO SIDELINES IN THE CULTURE WAR

The digital network has made the cost of communication small; this means that large organizations and institutions can quickly find themselves in a losing battle against the formerly powerless. It is important to note that this dynamic cuts both ways. The ability for smaller players within the network to have a louder voice may empower activists in a totalitarian regime while also enabling small nefarious groups to undermine stable democracies. The same tools can allow a victim to expose the wrongdoing of a large organization as well as a toxic troll to wreak havoc within a healthy institution.

For public-facing organizations and institutions, this creates a hazardous environment. Institutions that try to stay out of the conflicts of the networked world find themselves being drawn into culture war battles in the digital network, calibrated to react to the smallest inputs. Even silence can be interpreted as a form of communication. Why does this happen? Networks change the rules of communication.

The centralized organizations of the Industrial Age held communications dominance. Corporations could afford expensive advertising, well-funded institutions could access mass media to communicate, and organizations could produce their newspapers, magazines, and materials. Denominations and influential churches also maintained communications dominance, spreading their values and vision through books, broadcasts, magazines, and resources. The structure of the media landscape enabled them to pursue their plans of discipleship and mission with an informational monopoly.

The danger for institutions that held communications dominance was that they could lose touch with public opinion. The field of public relations taught organizations and corporations to manage their public image by being receptive to the opinion of the masses. Public relations baked into organizations a deep sensitivity to and fear of negative feedback. This sensitivity is still present in most organizations. However, with the advent of social media, the public possesses access to exponentially stronger feedback loops. Any person with access to the internet can comment on a multinational corporation's Facebook page for no cost. Activists of all persuasions and beliefs have noted the hypersensitivity and reactivity of our digital world and use this to their advantage, applying pressure on larger organizations through online feedback to advance their goals.

This kind of pressure can be used against a variety of opponents. In this horizontal dynamic, activists and individuals use the network to minimize their opponents' power. This is what we call cancel culture, a tactic employed both by the political left and right (and a growing number of other groups). The goal of cancel culture is not to throw someone into jail but rather to exclude them from the network. Cancel culture is less a top-down affair as it is a horizontal tactic of networked informational war. It's a privatized form of censorship, working as a form of freelance moral enforcement in the global network. It's the digital equivalent of the vigilante groups established on the chaotic frontier of the early American West, executing justice in what they see as a lawless environment.

Even the most committed believer will consume only a fraction of the information and input from their church compared to what they consume via podcasts, YouTube, and Netflix.

In a decentralized world, organizations, institutions, and churches can find themselves entangled in cultural battles as groups within their ranks create new feedback loops of discontent. Organizations and institutions contain boundaries and borders. However, in a network, there are few boundaries. Networks bring what was far close and what was formerly outside inside.

THERE IS NO NEUTRAL GROUND IN A NETWORK

In our previous phase, we often worried that Christians would hide away from the world in a Christian bubble, distracted with their doctrinal squabbles. This scenario is now smashed. The network's connectivity and the disruptions that decentralization brings mean that there is no place to stand apart from the world. Cultural and political battles crash into congregations and denominations, replacing the in-house doctrinal squabbles and worship wars of the past.

In the networked world, even the most committed believer will consume only a fraction of the information and input from their church compared to what they consume via podcasts, YouTube, and Netflix. The digital network is now our primary formational environment. It shapes our opinions, values, and worldview. Today, the average churchgoer will Google a problem before they approach their pastor. The digital network is the primary shaper of their theological, political, and cultural worldview.

David Kinnaman and Mark Matlock warn that "screens *disciple*."[2] They note that this trend is occurring with "even those who are very committed—[they] are busier than ever, attend church less frequently, and have many options for socializing outside a faith community."[3] This creates a new and challenging environment for the church. A congregation may be physically present within their church, but their primary influence comes from the digital networks to which they are connected. These digital networks may be political, cultural, or theological. In most churches, there are now multiple external networks present within congregations, facilitating internal feedback loops in which the agendas and objectives of external networks are advanced. Those preaching and communicating can find themselves outmaneuvered by one or many competing factions within their church that advance the goals and worldview of outside networks.

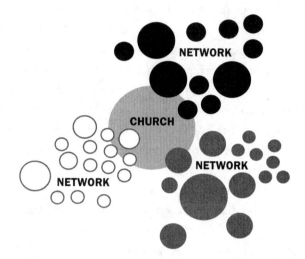

These outside networks could be political movements, conspiracy theories, nationalist movements, social networks, causes, or migrant diasporas.

With outside networks becoming the primary shaper of those we lead, the social dynamic within our churches and Christian organizations has become enflamed. Even before the effects of the internet intensified this pattern, Edwin Friedman understood how humans trend toward anxiety and the challenge this presented to leaders.

ANXIETY GOES VIRAL

Friedman noted that "chronic anxiety is systemic; it is deeper and more embracing than community nervousness. Rather than something that resides within the psyche of each one, it is something that can envelop, if not actually connect, people."[4] This means that despite how much we try and rationally think through issues, we will find ourselves enveloped within a system of chronic anxiety. Just as an individual may find themselves overcome by an infection to the point of becoming feverishly unwell, Friedman's diagnosis of contemporary society was that it too had become profoundly sick and was feverish with anxiety.

> **KEY IDEA:** *Anxiety flows virally through social networks, enveloping institutions in unhealthy emotions.*

HERDING

As a system overrun by anxiety becomes more reactive, it trends toward what Friedman labeled a herd instinct, in which "everyone will be emotionally fused with everyone else."[5] This creates a dynamic in which "the desire for good feelings rather than progress will on its own promote togetherness over individuality."[6] With the system rearranging itself to cater to the most emotionally unhealthy, those who wish to reflect, gain some distance to find perspective, or practice emotional health will pose a threat.

For example, a leader who decides to confront the issue of toxic political polarization within those they lead will often find others cautioning against such a remedy, instead recommending that leaders avoid upsetting either side.

Those wishing to chart a healthier direction will face tremendous pressure to adapt to the low emotional health that has captured the system. Any goals or programs of an institution that becomes overtaken by chronic anxiety will be replaced by the task of keeping the most dysfunctional members happy. Friedman saw this dynamic as cultlike. In this scenario, appeals to unity and inclusivity are masquerades to resist growth and any attempts at emotional renewal. Eventually, the herd instinct, rooted in emotional toxicity, will lead to fragmentation and falling out, as dysfunctional members of the system turn on each other.

REACTIVITY

As a network is swamped by chronic anxiety, it is marked by reactivity. Those within the system no longer act rationally, but rather, high emotion becomes the dominant form of interaction. The system's focus is directed toward the most emotionally immature and reactive members. Those who are more mature and healthy begin to adapt their behavior to appease the most irrational and unhealthy. This creates a scenario where the most emotionally unhealthy and immature members in the system become de facto leaders, shaping the emotional landscape with the focus on their negative behavior and what they see as the negative behavior of others. The anxiety present envelops the vision of the organization within the system.

In a chronically anxious system, Friedman argued, "The more aggressive members are in a perpetually argumentative stance, and the more passive are in a constant state of flinch."[7] Conflict and retreat become the dominant modes of engagement with others. It becomes nearly impossible to gain any distance from an issue; reaction, hurt, and high emotions replace contemplation and thoughtfulness. Reflection is replaced by reactivity.

We see this mood everywhere today—social media interactions, political discourse, even within churches and families. As tools for gaining space and relief from an issue, humor, irony, and satire are lost. To the emotionally immature, everything becomes at best a slight, at worst a direct assault. Feelings become all-powerful and fragile all at the same time. Conflict, sexual activity, and even violence become normative forms of social engagement and interaction within a chronically anxious system's network of human relationships.

It becomes nearly impossible for the healthier members of a system or its leadership to see the bigger issue and tackle systemic issues because the focus is brought back to the latest crisis and the feverish emotional responses that are swamping the network. Life-saving surgery can never occur because all the focus is on immediate pain management. The focus of the system cycles rapidly through continual crises. A marker of the emotionally unhealthy is a lack of personal boundaries and a disrespect of individual, institutional, and socially accepted boundaries. This enables chronic dysfunction and emotional toxicity to spread virally throughout the system.

Friedman observed that the kind of toxic behavior associated with chronically anxious and emotionally unhealthy families was seeping out of the family unit and into community organizations, public institutions, the business world, and even communities of faith. The online world has created an even larger platform for this behavior to spread far and wide within the global system. Our digital network acts like a super-spreading agent of anxiety within the already existing relational and social networks.

FRIEDMAN'S SOLUTION

To this challenge, Friedman proposed a novel and radical leadership solution. Traditionally our understanding is that leaders leverage influence and inspire and direct others through unique attributes.

We imagine that someone is suited to leadership because of their charisma, drive, intelligence, training, or achievements. Instead, Friedman argued that the most vital attribute to lead, especially in anxious human environments and systems, was a non-anxious presence. Thus, the leader's chief tool of influence is their presence.

Think of it this way. You are in a room with a large group listening to a lecture given by officials. Halfway through the presentation, smoke begins to fill the space. Someone screams, "FIRE!" Panic begins to grip the room. The exit seems to be blocked. All eyes turn to the officials at the front of the room. Yet they also seem to be so overcome with panic that they cry, scream, and shake. Then a woman emerges from the crowd, steadily walking up to the podium. In a calm but firm voice, she assures everyone that there is another exit at the back of the room, declares that everything will be okay, and asks people to leave via the rear door in a calm and orderly manner. In this scenario, who is the leader? Before the smoke appeared, most people would have seen the officials standing at the front of the room as the leaders. However, once the crisis arrived and panic and anxiety swept through the room, the calm and non-anxious woman who addressed the crowd would be seen by most as the leader. The lesson? In an anxious, crisis-driven environment, the leadership leverage comes from a non-anxious presence.

In an anxious, crisis-driven environment, the leadership leverage comes from a non-anxious presence.

KEY IDEA: *In anxious environments, leaders leverage influence through being a non-anxious presence.*

The roots of Friedman's solution of the non-anxious presence can be found in his understanding of systems thinking. For Friedman, the non-anxious leader played the role within an emotionally unhealthy social system akin to the role that white blood cells play in the human body, fighting infection and bringing the system back to health. Just as anxiety can multiply throughout a system, Friedman argued that non-anxiousness could similarly reset a system. "Leaders function as the immune systems of the institutions they lead—not because they ward off enemies but because they supply the ingredients for the system's integrity,"[8] Friedman counsels.

However, to do this, the leader who wishes to operate as a non-anxious presence within an emotionally unhealthy system must understand a fundamental principle. So vital was this principle that Friedman labeled it "the keys to the kingdom." The fundamental principle was to remain present within the unhealthy environment while enduring the sabotage, backlash, and undermining that leaders inevitably face when trying to act as non-anxious presences in anxious social systems.

As the leader faces this backlash, the great danger is that anxiety will rise within them, enveloping them and making them part of the problem rather than the solution. The leader would then have what Friedman labeled as a "Failure of Nerve." Therefore, leaders who wish to be a non-anxious presence must keep their nerve and push through the backlash, sabotage, betrayal from friends and colleagues, criticism, and emotional pain, and keep growing toward the higher vision in a non-anxious way.

Pushing past the pain and backlash toward the greater goal is something very few of us have been prepared for or trained to do. So instead, when facing the difficulty of leading within the gray zone, many take the off-ramp into another zone—the comfort zone— which we will learn about in the next chapter.

RECAP: THREE KEY TAKEAWAYS

- A more connected world is a more conflicted and therefore anxious world.

- Anxiety flows virally through social networks, enveloping institutions in unhealthy emotions.

- In anxious environments, leaders leverage influence through being a non-anxious presence.

CHAPTER 8

From the Gray Zone to the Comfort Zone

As we have learned, one of the societal roles of institutions was to absorb anxiety. However, with the devaluing and disappearance of institutions, individuals were left to absorb the culture's anxiety, which means that anxiety grows exponentially in a gray zone. As a result, leaders must lead anxious individuals while at the same time dealing with the wave of cultural anxiety, which crashes into the leader's personal life. This task is made even more difficult in a networked world of conflict and culture war.

Leading in the gray zone means navigating a challenging environment. This creates anxiety, which prevents the activation of spiritual growth. Yet as we will find in the economy of God, challenge carries a different value. It becomes a precious resource. The presence of God transforms challenge into spiritual growth.

Yet many can miss out on the spiritual growth that occurs in times of challenge. When something is challenging or difficult, we often retreat. Our culture has created the idea of comfort zones, the idea we can be both successful while avoiding discomfort. However, this myth prevents us from growing and moving into renewal.

KEY IDEA: *Anxiety prevents the activation of the seeds of renewal. However, challenge activates spiritual growth.*

STRONGHOLDS PROTECT THE PROCESS OF GROWTH

In the ancient world, nomads became village dwellers as the recurring problem of scarcity drove them to learn the ways of agriculture. The planting of seeds to harvest crops ensured a regular food supply. However, the process of growth required patience and dedication. Suppose those planting seeds wished to enjoy the fruit of their labors. They needed to stay close to the process of growth.

A village that grew around crops produced constant food and left farmers vulnerable to the violently impatient, who raided for food and supplies. Thus walls were built to protect crops, leading to villages becoming walled towns and fortified cities. This reveals an important truth. Not only do we build strongholds to absorb our anxiety but we also make strongholds because we are anxious about the process of growth. We want to protect what we have seeded.

However, as strongholds grew in strength and sophistication, many citizens became distanced from the process of growth. As cities and nations developed in their agricultural ability, crops and cattle became domesticated. In turn, the citizens of cities would also become domesticated. The production of food became an assumed fact of life—growth taken for granted. The distance expanded between the process of growth and the enjoyment of the fruit. Anxiety about scarcity, and the production of growth, is then replaced by a sense of entitlement.

KEY IDEA: *Instead of educating us in the process of growth, strongholds create entitlement in us. We expect fruit without the work that produces growth.*

THE STRONGHOLD OF SELF

Our mental image of a stronghold is most likely a castle—the fortified structures that dotted the medieval European landscape. Previously, only the state was permitted to build fortifications. However, as the decline of Rome ended, the ancient era and the gray zone of the Dark Ages began. People feared a return of disorder and chaos. So ordinary citizens started building protective structures. The first castles sprang up in the Italian lands once ruled by the all-powerful hand of Caesar. They contained a potential chieftain or king. As the power of Caesar and the Roman Empire faded and was delegitimized, a vast patchwork of tiny kingdoms and castles emerged.[1]

This leads us to an important lesson. As significant strongholds lose legitimacy, they birth smaller strongholds. As this happens, a transfer of power and authority occurs downwards, explaining how individualism can be understood as the creation of small strongholds of the self in our day.

In his study of the development of urban life, Lewis Mumford commented that as a city grew in size, the forms of village life, the sense of neighborliness and group identity, are diminished by the city's growth. "The 'We' becomes a buzzing swarm of 'I's.'"[2] The stronghold of the modern city births the stronghold of self—the contemporary individual.

The seeds of the contemporary individual self were sown and sprouted in Europe. The growing space afforded by the American continent ensured rapid and radical growth in how individuals understood themselves. The individualist self began to resemble the American century's power, form, and structure in miniature form. The self became its own kind of stronghold, mimicking the design of a stronghold.

Anything that could breach the walls of the stronghold of self, and compromise its inner freedom, becomes a danger.

The self receives greater autonomy. However, the price for this autonomy means it also must manage its anxiety. The stronghold of self must navigate the competitive nature of society. It finds connection as social ties become weaker. Without the direction of accepted social norms, the self must continually practice content risk analysis while assessing the diversity of choice that contemporary life brings. Rejecting the defining narratives of the broader social stronghold, the stronghold of self must generate its self-defining narratives.

Anything that could breach the walls of the stronghold of self, and compromise its inner freedom, becomes a danger. Relationships and responsibility, in particular, pose a specific threat to the self as a stronghold. Relationships are still valued and pursued but only if they remain superficial, requiring little sacrifice from us. Thus walls needed to be erected to protect the self. Just as significant strongholds project power, so does the self as a stronghold. The stronghold of self works to project its will and desire in the world, seeking the continual expansion of its personal freedom.

Sociologist Ronald Inglehart has noted that a "society's culture is shaped by the extent to which its people grow up feeling that survival is secure or insecure."[3] Societies of scarcity shape us differently than societies of abundance, which assume survival. Inglehart argues that the values held by individuals in societies of abundance trend toward self-expression rather than group identity, rights rather than responsibilities, and secular rather than religious frameworks.

STRONGHOLDS AND COMFORT ZONES

The fruit most valued by the contemporary stronghold of self is comfort. In the contemporary world, feeling good is the expected normative state of being. When one doesn't experience good feelings—if a task is unpleasant, if a relationship goes through a difficult period, if a job is tough—it is taken as a signal that something is wrong, or that something is wrong with you. The absence of good feelings becomes an amber warning light.

This drive to find a place of ease and good feelings is known as a comfort zone. We create a kind of stronghold based on feeling comfortable, at ease, and unchallenged by external distractions, disruptions, and intrusions. Success is maintaining the emotional balance of the comfort zone. However, this approach to life is built on a religious assumption that the stronghold can deliver a type of environment that facilitates a life that feasts on the fruit of comfort.

THE SECULAR SABBATH

In the book of Genesis, we find God resting on the seventh day, having brought order to the unformed chaos of the world. Biblical scholar John Walton comments on the rest of God on the seventh day: "We can discern that resting pertains to the security and stability found in the equilibrium of an ordered system."[4] God, as the ruler of the earth, has defeated chaos and brought order. Why? So that humans will have a functional, orderly system in which to work and worship. Humans are hardwired by God to desire functionality and order to fulfill our God-given roles.

When we presume that we live in orderly, stable, and predictable environments, we presume that the stronghold in which we live has achieved a secular sabbath. They have defeated the forces of chaos and have initiated a functioning and ongoing rule and reign over chaos. We may still presume chaos and disorder exist in the world, but it happens "over there" or to other people. We presume that the secular sabbath is triumphant where we operate and function and that the primary function of the stronghold will continue, enabling us to live in the comfort zone. Yet this belief in a kind of secular sabbath leads to a tension.

Psychologist Dan McAdams has studied the unique formation of the "American self." He notes that the stronghold of self contains a contradiction: "To claim that one's life is mainly a matter of individual self-making is itself a strong cultural statement, reflecting the dominant cultural norm of American individualism." This means that, ironically, it is the collective values of the American century that promotes the idea that "self and culture have rather little to do with each other."[5] This contradiction creates an unstable dynamic in which the self pursues authority apart from the larger stronghold, yet at the same time is dependent on its ability to ensure a society of abundance. This means that comfort zones are dependent on strongholds and their ability to deliver us comfort and ease.

KEY IDEA: *Our personal strongholds, which seek autonomy, depend on the social strongholds that give us security.*

This balance can be kept, albeit precariously, while the stronghold maintains its dominance. However, individuals within a stronghold reject its authority and instead take control and centralize power within themselves. As a result, the legitimacy and effectiveness of the larger stronghold are reduced. This pattern is accelerating as the effects of decentralization become more pronounced. The great challenge of many Western nations is coherence in the face of increasing individualism and a dizzying diversity of opinion, in which consensus becomes nearly impossible. Strongholds such as states, institutions, and churches are buckling under the challenge of our decentralizing moment.

If indeed the American century birthed and sustained the American concept of self, the passing of the American century will likely result in the demise of the American stronghold of the self.

Leaders move people toward growth. Comfort zones insulate us from development. As we will learn in the next chapter, this is not only true for the people we lead but for leaders as well.

RECAP: THREE KEY TAKEAWAYS

- Anxiety prevents the activation of the seeds of renewal, while challenge activates spiritual growth.

- Instead of educating us in the process of growth, strongholds create a sense of entitlement in which we expect fruit without growth.

- Our personal strongholds, which seek autonomy, depend on the social strongholds that give us security.

CHAPTER 9

Leading from the Comfort Zone

Christian leadership is leading people into growth so that they may grow in Christlikeness. Growth, however, involves understanding that discomfort and pain are part of life and can be used by God to grow us. As we have learned, unhealthy individuals and systems make comfort and ease their highest value and thus do everything to avoid discomfort and pain. Management consultant Judith Bardwick noted that organizations, nations, and institutions faced danger when they became masters of their field, the danger of the comfort zone.[1] This means that they hold ease, comfort, and good feelings above growth. The choice to prioritize comfort, ease, and good feelings above growth is the choice to embrace and accept personal, spiritual, and emotional immaturity.

COMFORT ZONE LEADERSHIP

We learned in chapter 2 that God has seeded the world with renewal. Leaders are seed carriers. The first seeds of renewal are activated in their lives. As my friend Terry Walling says, "Personal renewal leads to corporate change." This is a pattern we see throughout history, as a process of growth in the leader becomes a foretaste of the growth and renewal that will occur in the people. However, the personal renewal that leads to corporate change can become short-circuited. How? When the leader gives in to the temptation to retreat into a comfort zone, where we continue to lead but from a space in which walls are erected to keep out that which is difficult and painful.

Friedman observed that "there is no way out of a chronic condition unless one is willing to go through an acute, temporarily more painful, phase."[2] For change to occur, the leader must enter into a process of growth, knowing that the process will lead through some uncomfortable terrain. We know that leading is often painful and challenging. Yet we also live in the age of Instagram influencer pastors, some of whom use social media to advance ministry and unintentionally spread a myth: that we can lead while staying within a comfort zone. This can lead us into the error of believing that success in ministry is leading well and feeling good all the time. This dynamic creates congregations that live within their comfort zones, led by leaders who wish to preserve their comfort zones.

KEY IDEA: *Churches and Christian organizations that have been overtaken by chronic anxiety will resist growth.*

Chronically anxious systems resist leaders who try to move toward growth. While sometimes this manifests in outright attack and undermining, resistance to growth can occur in the form of flattery. Anxiety leads us to look for approval. Thus, leaders in anxious systems can find themselves susceptible to flattery. We can fall into the temptation not to lead people toward growth but rather manage their good feelings. The goalposts can subtly shift from growing a church or organization toward health and growth to ensuring that the congregation is happy and comfortable.

Friedman argued that anxious leaders could turn to quick-fix solutions, which offer a pain-free and rapid exit from that which ails us in anxious environments. This is an important insight. The leader who applies quick-fix solutions, even when they fail to address the root issues we genuinely face and fail to lead us toward growth, will be championed. Good communicators who home in on a quick-fix solution, applying it seemingly successfully in their context, may even find broad audiences beyond their organization, growing platform, and even fame, becoming caught up in a celebrity circuit that delivers approval and celebrates quick-fix solutions. The true root of our issues is never addressed, and deep, renewing growth is not advanced.

Now more than any other time in the church's history, there is no shortage of quick fixes on offer that promise us growth without pain. Turkish writer Zeynep Tufekci[3] makes the point that the kind of platform of influence that social media enables us to build can rapidly create events and movements that appear with a bang. These can be large in number and impressive, usually coalescing quickly around the promise of offering a solution, which then disappears in a moment. The Occupy movement that emerged rapidly in the wake of the global financial movement began impressively, yet struggled to coalsesce into a coherent opposition to the destructive economic practices it opposed.

Tufekci argues that in the past, movements were built slowly over time. Leaders would spend years building up a critical mass, pouring out blood, sweat, and tears, and eventually—a movement was formed with the mission and capacity to advance change. However, today we can create an event, gather a crowd, or amass an audience online quickly. Then, over time, like a flash mob dissipating, the promise slowly evaporates, leaving little changed. Yet what remains is the promise that we can find shortcuts to success without the pain of growth. The wilderness is filled with many mirages.

> **KEY IDEA:** *Christian culture can offer us models of leading from the comfort zone, which can look successful from earthly metrics but fail to lead people into spiritual growth.*

THE COMFORT ZONE PUSHES US INTO FANTASY

We create comfort zones to keep the anxiety out; we also make them protect our autonomy. However, in the gray zone, we discover we possess less freedom than our ideology of individualism promises. This can push us further into fantasy to find more freedom. As individuals and as a society, we increasingly spawn and prefer fantasy environments. From Instagram accounts where everyone looks better in their photos than they do in real life, to the political echochambers of Twitter, in which algorithms ensure that everyone on your timeline agrees with your politics, to the forthcoming virtual reality playgrounds of the metaverse.

The frontier myth seeded within the American century's

imagination an ever-expanding quest to discover more freedom. However, in a world of brokenness, sin, and limitations, this is impossible. Humans are not divine. At some point, the endless quest for freedom will run up against the boundaries of reality. For example, we can fight the aging process with full arsenal of weapons that the modern cosmetic industry provides us, but eventually we all must face the reality that human aging marks us physically.

However, the Portuguese writer Bruno Macaes argues that faced with the limitations of reality, the new American frontier is the frontier between reality and fantasy. For when our freedom runs into reality, fantasy promises us the possibility of expanding our freedom beyond its natural boundaries.[4] Science fiction author Philip K. Dick, commenting in the 1970s, sensed how fantasy would shape the future of society, warning that "fake realities will create fake humans," which will lead to a disastrous cascade of crises in which "fake humans will generate fake reality and then sell them to other humans, turning them, eventually, into forgeries of themselves."

The endgame of such a process would be that society would transform into "a very large version of Disneyland."[5] Cultural critic Kurt Andersen notes that this warning has become true in our day, as fantasy is pursued at a mass scale, creating an expansive "fantasy-industrial complex,"[6] a vast cultural and social machinery that spawns fantasies and fantasy lives. Our malls, computer games, advertisement-filled airports, and even political rallies increasingly seem to be cut from the same cloth and detached from reality, instead offering us a wide swathe of utopian fantasies.

Furnished with fantasies, the contemporary comfort zone has become a different kind of stronghold, built not just to keep out anxiety but also to protect us from reality. Why? Because reality makes us anxious. We cannot shape reality to our wishes. As a result, our faith in freedom and the power of our autonomy is shattered.

Fantasy has spawned false visions of life and leadership. Comfort zones furnished with fantasy develop fragile individuals, leaders, and organizations, as their fantasies are continually shattered by reality. A lack of connection with reality creates a lack of resilience.

GRAY ZONES ARE THE WILDERNESS

The gift of gray zones is that they bring us back to reality. They shatter illusions. They pierce the walls and get around the battlements of our strongholds of fantasy and comfort. Without an actual realization of our true state, our weakness and brokenness, our need for God's renewing grace, we cannot grow. Fantasy subverts and prevents growth. In a fantasy world, the only thing you can develop is more fantasies. The painful encounter with reality we experience in our gray zone moment opens up the possibility of encountering the deeper work God wishes to do within us.

The gray zone frightens us. It reminds us of the primal chaos in a world that threatens to overwhelm us. It carries echoes of the wilderness, exposing our lack of control over the world and shattering our illusions and our idolatrous belief that we can live a life without pain. Yet Scripture reframes the role of the wilderness for us. The in-between gray zone of the wilderness is a recurring theme within the Bible. Without God, wildernesses, both literal and figurative, are terrible places. With God, they become tools in our Savior's hands. Schools of spiritual growth.

Without an actual realization of our true state, our weakness and brokenness, our need for God's renewing grace, we cannot grow.

The wilderness reveals the direction of our hearts. Our character is indeed shown in moments of challenge. Outside the protective walls of our strongholds, we find out who we are. Do we grumble, wishing to return to Egypt, or do we praise in the desert? Do we rebel or depend? Do we starve or eat manna? Do we build a golden calf or follow the pillar of cloud?

Wilderness is the place of testing. We don't usually associate testing with spiritual growth. For most people, it brings up memories of school, exams, and papers. The testing we encounter in the biblical imagination is different. It is more akin to an intense process of spiritual growth in which God both seeks and forms people after His own heart,[7] people who want what He wants, who wish to be shaped by Him. Set apart for His purposes.

The testing in Scripture is more akin to how a personal trainer at a gym may take a new client through an initial fitness test to assess the starting point of where they are physically and where they need to improve. The initial test for many people can be humbling. They are revealing how we pridefully overestimated our abilities. Yet this is part of a more extensive and beneficial process. The client will then be given a tailored program designed to grow them over time with the help of the trainer, who guides them into a healthy and fit person. In spiritual testing, our actual spiritual state is revealed in all its inadequacy and failings. This, however, is part of a broader strategy of spiritual growth.

Deuteronomy explains how He uses the wilderness to test us and grow us:

> "Remember how the LORD your God led you through the wilderness for these forty years, humbling you and testing you to prove your character, and to find out whether or not you would obey

his commands. Yes, he humbled you by letting you go hungry and then feeding you with manna, a food previously unknown to you and your ancestors. He did it to teach you that people do not live by bread alone; rather, we live by every word that comes from the mouth of the LORD." (Deut. 8:2–4 NLT)

What about those who have strayed from God's path, those whose eyes have veered in idolatrous directions? Are such people simply to die of spiritual thirst in the desert? No, the opposite is true. God uses the wilderness to win many back when they stray. With God, streams of living water appear in the desert.

THE WILDERNESS IS WHERE HE WINS US BACK AND GIVES US GOLD

In Scripture, we encounter the prophet Hosea, whose unfaithful wife strays from him. To win her heart back, he takes her to the desert places. The romantic imagery of the book points to a larger spiritual truth in which Hosea represents God, and Gomer, his wife, the unfaithful people who stray from His way. Speaking of the wilderness, the Lord says in Hosea 2,

> "But then I will win her back once again. I will lead her into the desert and speak tenderly to her there. I will return her vineyards to her and transform the Valley of Trouble into a gateway of hope. She will give herself to me there, as she did long ago when she was young, when I freed her from her captivity in Egypt." (Hos. 2:14–15 NLT)

The language of this passage reframes the wilderness experience that Israel endured after they escaped from captivity in Egypt with honeymoon imagery. The wilderness is where He woos. The gray zone is where He wins our hearts back to Him, where He turns a valley of trouble into a gateway of hope.

This means that the testing, the difficulty and the challenge of the wilderness, and our contemporary challenging gray zone moment is where we encounter God's love for us. He allows us to move through difficult moments. To live in confronting places. He tests us because He loves us enough to grow us; this means we must reevaluate our gray zone moment as a place ripe with the potential for spiritual growth.

Australia is a huge country, the size of the continental United States, but with a population of only twenty-five million people. The majority of Australians live hugging the coast, staying close to the water. Most of Australia is desert. Yet despite all of this barren land, Australia is a wealthy country. Its citizens are some of the most affluent in the world. Why? Because Australia possesses an incredible reserve of natural resources, from iron ore, gold, aluminum, coal, oil, gas, and uranium, exported at a significant profit. The vast majority of these resources are not found in the comfortable and green coastal environment where most Australians live. They lie deep under the harsh desert places.

Australia's enviable lifestyle and wealth and predominantly urban lifestyle of comfort is only made possible by the minority. The miners and those in the resources industry head out into the extreme and often dangerous environments and bring back their riches. This illustrates a fundamental spiritual truth for us. To get the gold, you have to go into the wilderness.

Disciples, those who take significant ground for the kingdom, leave the greenery, the beaches, and the comfort zones of the coastline. They are the minority who head out into the desert. To bring back the spiritual resources, the gold that is found in hard ground.

Comfort zones are poor soil in which to activate seeds of growth and renewal. To learn more, let's return to the island of Krakatoa.

SEEDS LIE IN DORMANCY

For the scorched earth of Krakatoa to spring back into life, something more than simply the transportation of seeds by birds, wind, and sea currents to the island needed to occur. In order to grow, seeds must be activated. Activation occurs when seeds are placed in the right environment, which triggers their growth. Without activation, seeds will lie dormant; this explains why, for a period, the botanists and explorers who ventured onto Krakatoa could see no sign of life. Then, however, an incredible explosion of renewal and life occurred. What seemed like nothingness and death was a period of dormancy.

There are many dreams for the church, for the world, for your life, that may seem dead at the moment. The seed reminds us not to mistake dormancy for death.

Seeds teach us this lesson. The oldest seed ever to be germinated was discovered in the ruins of King Herod's palace at Masada in Israel. In 2008, a group of researchers planted the seed in soil. Amazingly this two-thousand-year-old seed germinated, growing into a palm plant.[8]

Seeds can preserve and transport life over great times and distances, encasing potential within their tiny form. Contained within them is everything that they will be. Seeds wait to expand into their full potential in the right environment. There are many dreams for the church, for the world, for your life, that may seem dead at the moment. The seed reminds us not to mistake dormancy for death.

FROM DORMANCY TO ACTIVATION

However, for this growth to be released, the seed must be roused from its dormancy. It must begin a process of rapid growth. This process of exponential development can only start when the seed is placed in the right environment to trigger its growth. Seeds move from dormancy to activation when they're placed in the right soil. The chemicals in the outer coat of the seed sense when it's in nutrient-rich soil. Even after two thousand years, a message is sent that this is the place in which it's safe to grow. The potential of the seed is released, and life bursts forth.

Jesus taught His disciples in the parable of the sower that for a seed to release its exponential potential, to produce "a crop—a hundred, sixty or thirty times what was sown" (Matt. 13:8), the seed must be placed in good soil. Good soil, according to Jesus, is when someone hears the Word and grasps the fullness of its meaning. In contrast, a far more challenging environment for growing seeds is an environment of worldly comforts and wealth, which leads to anxiety.

ANXIETY PREVENTS ACTIVATION

We have learned that God seeds every season with His Word. When leaders hear this Word, understand it, and through faith live it, renewal and kingdom life is released into the world. For seeds to unleash the power of exponential growth within them, they must be activated into development. We also have learned that God seeds even the most difficult of seasons with leaders. Personal renewal in the lives of leaders brings about corporate change. Leaders are conduits of renewal, embodying the kingdom transformation to come. They live the next season that God will bring. Leaders live the hope to come, becoming hinges to God's future.

Yet often these leaders lie dormant, waiting to be activated. However, lousy soil works against activation. Jesus taught that the worries of this life are bad soil, working against kingdom activation. It is my experience, talking to leaders from across the globe, that by far the dominant bad soil, preventing kingdom activation and leaving countless numbers of leaders in dormancy, is the concerns of the world that Jesus warned of.

To make this as clear as I can, it's the stronghold of self. The pursuit of good feelings. The assumption is that the stronghold of our world is there to deliver you the good fruit of a pleasurable life. These factors are leaving a whole cohort of leaders dormant: awaiting an activation that will never come while they stay in their comfort zones. Because if you are going to grow in spiritual authority, the seed of renewal must be activated within you.

We understand the concept of earthly authority, given to us by governments, workplaces, or even families. Spiritual authority emerges from heaven. It is conferred on us by God as we walk in alignment with His will. To grow in spiritual authority, we are going to have to step outside of our comfort zones and break away from the grip of the myth that life is going wrong when we are not feeling good.

KEY IDEA: *To grow, and lead others into growth, you must abandon the myth that leading will always feel good. Comfort zones insulate us against growth; gray zones activate us into spiritual growth when we say yes to God's invitation to grow with Him.*

Returning to Krakatoa. It is of note that some of the first trees to appear upon Anak Krakatoa were "a pine-like tree that the Australians named (for its resemblance to the lush plumage of their native cassowary bird) the casuarina,"[9] writes Simon Winchester. The cassowary is a mysterious and visually striking bird. The flightless cassowary lives deep in the Northern Australian rainforest. A formidable foe, the cassowary can powerfully fight off large predators and has even killed humans with its giant talons. Intriguingly the cassowary also plays a part in germinating the seeds of a rare plant known as the Ryparosa. Ryparosa seeds have meager rates of germination. However, when a seed passes through the digestive system of the cassowary its potential to germinate is increased by up to 90 percent.[10] The extreme and challenging environment of the cassowary's acidic digestive system triggers growth within the seed.

There is a crucial lesson here: growth can be activated in dormant seeds when they are placed in unusual and challenging environments. The seed of renewal is activated in leaders in tough environments.

The most comfortable of environments from a temporal and earthly perspective are the worst environments for the seed of the kingdom to grow. "God values character and maturity much more than we humans do. Here is a fact: character and maturity are more important than comfort and ease," writes Rob Reimer. For the kingdom power laws of exponential spiritual growth to be activated, we need to grasp a counterintuitive truth. Hard places are good soil for kingdom seeds. Testing in the hard ground of the wilderness is difficult and often uncomfortable, yet it grows us. Reimer notes that "testing also gives us more capacity for God in our lives. By enduring hardship, God is going to make you have a stronger inner temple, which can contain more of his presence."[11] This truth reframes our gray zone moment.

While we may pine for more stable and predictable times, from a kingdom perspective, this time in history may be the kind of environment that activates a whole cohort of leaders hidden and waiting for activation, for God's presence turns our gray zone into a growth zone.

First, though, we must unlearn the leadership strategies formed in the previous era, which have left us ill-equipped to lead well in the complexity of the gray zone.

RECAP: THREE KEY TAKEAWAYS

- Churches and Christian organizations that have been over-taken by chronic anxiety will resist growth.

- Christian culture can offer us models of leading from the comfort zone, which can look successful from earthly metrics but fail to lead people into spiritual growth.

- To grow, and lead others into growth, you must abandon the myth that leading will always feel good. Comfort zones insulate us against growth; gray zones activate us into spiritual growth when we say yes to God's invitation to grow with Him.

CHAPTER 10

From Efficiency to Adaptation

In his classic book *Good Strategy/Bad Strategy*, Richard Rumelt lauds the strategic effectiveness of the American general Norman Schwarzkopf during the first Gulf War. Schwarzkopf faced a sizeable Iraqi Army led by Saddam Hussein, who was on home turf, and observers predicted a possibly long and deadly battle. In addition, Schwarzkopf confronted the challenge of leading a multinational force with competing interests as well as US forces, which contained various branches of the military that were engaged in significant competition with each other. Nevertheless, Schwarzkopf led the troops under his command to a victory that devastated the Iraqi Army. Rumelt notes that in the wake of the victory, commentators celebrated the strategic genius of the general. However, Schwarzkopf had effectively applied the first and most straightforward strategy outlined in the US army's field manual, which Rumelt informs us was available to anyone for only a few dollars.

What made Schwarzkopf's achievement remarkable, according to Rumelt, was that he took a complex organization, the multinational force that had gathered under the banner of Operation Desert

Storm, blocked out the competing voices, and made them work effectively. The message is that effective execution and doing things by the book beats complexity. According to this doctrine, effective leaders are successful when they wrestle a complex organization into shape and lead their organization in unified action toward what are considered the best practices.

However, by the Second Gulf War, the world had radically changed. Again the United States and its allies defeated the Iraqi Army rapidly and effectively. But as soon as President George W. Bush proclaimed the mission accomplished, coalition forces were engulfed in a bloody and complex gray zone insurgency. The first Gulf War was a "flip phone" conflict. The Iraqi insurgency was a smartphone war. New technology created a networked enemy that operated and thrived in a complex, chaotic gray zone environment.

Reflecting on the changed conditions encountered in the Second Gulf War, General Stanley McChrystal recounts that although possessing far greater resources, training, and materiel advantages, the forces under his command were losing to an enemy they should have dominated. However, McChrystal realized that what he was battling was less an enemy than a changing environment. "We were actually struggling to cope with an environment that was fundamentally different from anything we'd planned or trained for. The speed and interdependence of events had produced new dynamics that threatened to overwhelm the time-honored process and culture we'd built."[1]

McChrystal's words remind me of the sentiment of many pastors I spoke to as the axial shift of 2020 occurred. Pastors dealt with the reality of transitioning to digital church during the pandemic, coping with political division, internet misinformation, post-Christianity, and the complexities of social media. Ministry was already increasingly challenging before 2020. However, this new and confusing environment was like nothing they had ever seen or been trained for. As a result, many were ready to throw in the towel.

FROM A COMPLICATED WORLD
TO A COMPLEX WORLD

Computer scientist Ted Lewis notes that "the comparatively straightforward Industrial Revolution has morphed into an era of nonlinear change punctuated with tipping points. The machinery of the current century is a collection of interconnected complex, rather than smooth-running, systems. Gradual and linear change no longer happens. Instead, 'progress' moves in bursts—fits-and-starts marked by waves of unimaginable flashes, sparks, booms, bubbles, shocks, extremes, bombs, and leaps."[2] The Industrial Age created effective strategic and leadership solutions for a complicated world. However, we are moving into a complex world.

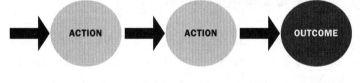

LINEAR

You may be wondering, aren't complicated and complex essentially the same thing? "The two aren't the same—and complexity isn't just complication on steroids,"[3] answers business writer Margaret Heffernan. A complex environment is more than just a complicated environment, with even more complications. The two are completely different beasts, with different rules and fundamentally different ways of behaving.

To offer an example, imagine you are asked to predict who will win a tennis match between two equally matched professionals. You could study their recent form, the type of court the match is being played on, or their current fitness and confidence levels. While it would be challenging, there is a logical set of steps you could undertake to give yourself a chance of predicting the winner. Now If we added another complication, making it a doubles match, the task of prediction would become more complicated. Yet it would still operate with the same rules of prediction you used for the singles match.

However, the task would move from a complicated one to a complex one if we added another three hundred players onto the court while allowing them to hit several hundred tennis balls at once. Prediction would become nearly impossible. The complicated system of the two professionals playing a match has turned into a complex system of hundreds of players, operating according to a different set of rules.

KEY IDEA: *We have moved from a complicated world to a complex world.*

Margaret Heffernan offers further definition: "Complicated environments are linear, follow rules, and are predictable; like an assembly line, they can be planned, managed, repeated, and controlled. They're maximized by routine and efficiency."[4] The linear world created by the Industrial Age was tuned for dealing with complicated problems; as mathematician Steven Strogatz notes, "Linear systems can be broken down into parts. Then each part can be solved separately and finally recombined to get the answer. This idea allows a fantastic simplification of complex problems." However, Strogatz offers a caveat, adding, "But many things in nature don't act this way."[5] Nature instead operates in a nonlinear fashion.

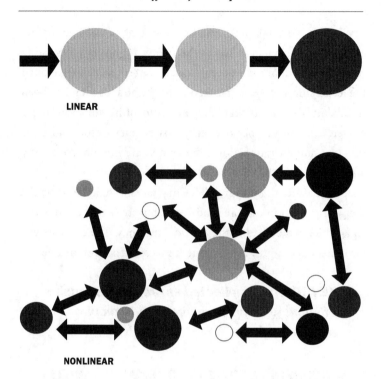

Nonlinearity is a difficult concept to grasp, since we are so attuned to linear thinking. In a complicated world, we tend to think of "events." We are engaged in linear projects and see change as an event that may interrupt our progress but ultimately can be managed. This is how many people approached the pandemic—initially interpreting it as an "event," a temporary interruption that may pause our linear projects for a period, but then life would return to normal as it was before. However, the pandemic was a complex event occurring within a complex world. It wasn't an interruption; it was an immersion. In a complicated world, events may interrupt our processes and projects. In a complex world, events envelop us in their processes. We must adapt to meet their challenge.

In Iraq, General McChrystal realized that he was fighting the environment as much as he was the enemy. He was now operating in a complex rather than complicated context, which enveloped the leadership strategies and tactics that he and his men had been trained in. He reflects that "the environment in which we found ourselves, a convergence of twenty-first-century factors and more timeless human interactions, demanded a dynamic, constantly adapting approach."[6] Such a gray zone environment demanded adaptable leaders. However, as McChrystal reflected, the army, like many organizations, favored the leadership styles of the Industrial Age, which worshiped at the altar of efficiency. The complex environment of our gray zone moment eats efficiency for breakfast.

KEY IDEA: *Complicated environments require efficiency. Complex environments require adaptability.*

WORSHIPING EFFICIENCY OVER ADAPTABILITY

General McChrystal had to undo some unhelpful mental concepts to lead those under his command into more adaptive leadership models. McChrystal saw the roots of much of our thinking regarding leadership, management, and efficiency leading back to the early management theorist and engineer Fredrick Taylor. Scholars have labeled Taylor as one of the most influential individuals in history who shaped our understanding of leading, working, and improving our daily lives. Taylor, a Quaker, never intended to influence how churches run, but as we will see, his influence on how the contemporary church operates is mammoth.

During the nineteenth century, and at the height of the

Industrial Revolution, Taylor devised a "scientific management theory of leadership"—now labeled Taylorism. Taylorism operates according to the following principles:

1. Determine your objective and goal.

2. Study the most efficient path to reach your goal.

3. Break that path into tasks, looking for the best practices to accomplish each task with maximum efficiency.

4. Delegate the task and best practices to specialists.

5. The specialists are managed by leaders, who supervise them, ensuring their compliance with best practices.

6. Reach the goal of efficiency and productivity. Rinse and repeat.

Planning, programs, prediction, and above all, efficiency became the way to success. Taylorism transformed leaders into managers who delegated tasks and supervised workers underneath them, managing them to achieve the various broken-up tasks in a linear fashion until the tasks are completed. According to historian Stephen Waring, "Taylorism effectively expressed and legitimized the developing attraction to centralization."[7] It became the model of centralized leadership for the centralized era of the American century, transforming leadership into the management of projects and processes.

The philosophy of Taylorism would also filter from the realm of work into the personal. The concept of personality profiles was introduced to assist managers in placing workers into specialized tasks within the process, which suited their abilities and temperaments. Personality profiles worked to offset the sense of depersonalization; many felt that Taylor's management theories reduced them to mere cogs within an extensive system of efficiency.

Taylor's techniques were also applied to the realm of personal improvement. Individuals were encouraged to "manage" their lives by aiming for personal development goals and creating "life projects," which were broken into achievable parts or habits to ensure productivity.

This thinking would also lead to the search for crucial practices, breakthrough techniques, and golden ideas, which would lead to success and productivity. Managers who had discovered an essential improvement in their field, or perhaps an efficient new program, could move outside of their organization or field to share their story of success, leveraging this critical insight into fame, wealth, and further success. Taylorism is why a whole genre of business books promotes and proclaims the authors' discovery of the singular component or program of success and promises success to the reader if they repeat the best practice in their particular context.

TAYLORISM AS THE CHIEF OPERATING SYSTEM

As the term suggests, *scientific management* looked to science to become more efficient. Science held a mechanical view of the universe and believed observation and measurement would enable the scientist to follow a linear sequence that allowed effective prediction. This was industrial thinking for an Industrial Age. This linking created beliefs that would act as leadership dogma:

- Linear thinking.

- The belief that change would happen gradually, logically, and sequentially.

- A belief that the more information and data we have, the more understanding we will have and the more empowered we will be.

- The assumption is that the essential environment we are operating in will remain stable.

- Outcomes will occur in a predictable range.

- Yesterday's solutions will continue to work tomorrow.

- The path to success is paved with efficiency.

These dogmas combined to create a kind of modern faith in which the developed world and its highest expression in the Industrial Age made a manageable, predictable, stable, efficient, and productive world. Assuming that the only thing that could upend our plans was a failure to plan and manage correctly, you would never imagine that a radical change in the environment, culture, or conditions would make such predictive planning impossible. Of course, you may be the variable, failing to fulfill your duty efficiently and thus losing productivity. Yet rarely would we assume that forces outside of your control would prevent you from planning your conference in a year. These assumptions take us to the foundational belief that undergirds Taylor's model of management, right up to its contemporary forms—definitive proof and tangible evidence. Yet these things work against the practice of faith.

TAYLORISM AND THE CONTEMPORARY CHURCH

Taylor's influence has been immense, particularly within the contemporary church and many other Christian ministries. The prime
tool for ministry, mission, and discipleship in most contemporary
Western churches is programming. We devise a ministry vision and
create a process of steps that takes participants in a linear direction
toward our desired outcome for them. We break up these programs
into segments and delegate tasks to staff and volunteers. We look to
other churches and contexts for best practices. We read books that
offer improvements that we could apply to our programs. We gauge
spiritual success via the productivity and outcomes of the linear
programs that we run. Much of spiritual leadership has become the
management of these programs and processes—the supervision of
those to whom segments of those processes have been delegated.
Often churches or ministries described as "successful" ultimately
are viewed in such a way because of their ability to run programs
with a high degree of efficiency.

All of this is classic Taylorism. I have even heard some Christian leaders argue that you don't need a pastor or a spiritual leader
in charge of a large church, but a competent manager from the
business world who can manage the processes and programs of
churches.

So is Taylorism wrong? Should churches and ministries cease
running programs? No. My church runs programs, and we intend
to continue doing so. Well-run programs can be a helpful tool for
kingdom work, particularly at scale. However, I am arguing that
in the gray zone that we are already in and will enter more fully,
Taylorist thinking will increasingly falter. Taylorism created the Industrial Age. It then became the chief operating system of success

within the Industrial Age. However, as we move away from the Industrial Age into the dynamics of a networked world, Taylorism will be a less effective tool. Taylorism likes stable environments that are linear and predictable.

Ultimately more than just designing and managing efficient programs, Taylorism is a mental model we use to view and make our way in the world. It was a set of lenses designed in the Industrial Age. This was made clear during the pandemic as I spoke to pastors who had asked me to help them think about how to respond to this disruption. I spoke with leaders who could not imagine that the pandemic might last more than a few weeks, primarily because of how this would disrupt or even prevent the continuation of their programs. I shared that I believed the pandemic may last for well over twelve months, possibly even two years of disruption and that it would be challenging to plan. I could see an almost physical reaction within some leaders, who simply could not imagine that planning and prediction would not be possible. Their received mental model was struggling with the emerging gray zone dynamics.

FROM TAYLORISM TO VIROLOGY

Nobel Prize winner Robert Schiller needed a new mental model. The American economist noted that the term *efficiency*, used to describe the natural order of financial markets, failed to capture the chaotic, nonlinear, and seemingly irrational ways in which the markets behaved. Schiller noticed new terminology was being used as people tried to capture the new dynamics of how the world economy operated. People spoke about new ideas that went "viral," economists warned about "contagions" within the markets, ideas about the market "spread like wildfire" through investors, causing investors to operate in "feverish" ways. The market was being spoken about in the language of epidemiology.

Although writing before the COVID-19 pandemic, Schiller recognized that the language of pandemics and epidemiology offered new ways to understand better how the market worked in a connected, complex global network: "It is helpful to consider how bacteria and viruses spread by contagion. The science of epidemiology offers valuable lessons." Schiller notes that "epidemiology has produced not one model but rather many different models that can be applied to different circumstances"[8] by studying viruses and the way they spread throughout networks, operating in surprising and nonlinear ways. Thus, epidemiologists needed to understand a much broader range of study in contrast to Taylorism, which reduced processes to their simplest forms, seeking the simplest solutions.

This side of the pandemic, fellow economist John Authers, recognizing Schiller's breakthrough thinking, noted, "After a year of watching charts of epidemics in different countries, comparing R-0 rates, cases, vaccinations, excess deaths and all the rest, and applying moving averages to sinister lines snaking across graphs, maybe we should now use our new-found familiarity with epidemiology to give us a new mental model."[9] In a sense, after following the pandemic closely, many of us now have become amateur epidemiologists, or at least have a grasp of the mental model.

Whereas before we could see the increasing complexity in the world, it often remained a dynamic "out there," not trickling down to the places in which we lived and the spaces in which we lead. However, with the arrival of COVID-19, the world received a crash course in the new dynamics. Thus epidemiology points us toward a different mental model that aligns more closely with how our gray zone operates.

THE FARMERS GET IT

Virology offers us a lesson on how complex environments operate. Spanish virologists Ricard Sole and Santiago Elena note that "viruses are complex systems"[10] that exist within the vast networked system scientists call the biosphere, or what is commonly known to most of us as nature. Nature itself is a complex (rather than complicated) system, which for most of human history has inspired both awe and terror in human beings. Those whose survival and livelihoods are linked to nature, such as farmers, understand its complexity, needing no lessons on how the slightest changes in nature can have significant effects. They understand how quickly we can be overwhelmed by the unexpected.

In the language and concepts of epidemiology, Robert Schiller found a better way to understand the dynamics and contours of our complex world. Stanley McChrystal also made the same upgrade in his thinking, finding that the concepts of immunology and infection explained what was happening in the gray zone battlefields of Iraq more than the industrial era concepts of leadership and management.[11] Viruses are warriors from the wilderness—small but powerful predators.

A worldwide pandemic offers a real-life lesson in how nature can get past the defenses and strategies of our strongholds, bringing the ways of the wilderness back into the city, undoing the controlled, complicated world the Industrial Age created. The complexity of nature places barriers on the freedom of the humans who live connected to it, plunging the modern world back into the gray zone. Nature reminds us of our limitations and the complexity of creation, destroying any hubris that we can conquer the world in our strength. Our weakness in the face of nature offers us the chance of a strategic reset. No longer can we assume we are in control—now we must learn to adapt.

PLAYING CHESS WITHOUT THE QUEEN

Viruses that survive and thrive, going viral, do so by rapidly adapting to their environments. They exist in what scientists label a fitness environment. The virus rapidly tests itself against the environment, looking for new routes of infection to ensure that the chain of transmission continues. This is why viruses like COVID-19 mutate into new, more transmissible, and deadly variants. This dynamic frustrates those used to seeing the world through the lens of Taylorism. The enemy that you faced yesterday, and for which you developed best practices to combat, can transform today, meaning that your best practices are now out of date and ineffective. As a result, you find yourself continually fighting the last war while losing the current one.

David Kilcullen,[12] an Australian professor of social sciences at the University of New South Wales, discovered that this kind of viruslike adaptation enabled the poorly resourced Iraqi insurgents to defeat the better-equipped coalition forces. Outgunned and outresourced, the Iraqi insurgents had to adapt rapidly and find the decisive asymmetry in their environment. The insurgents were in a desperate race to find the hidden advantages and power in their context. While they didn't have the training or superior resources of the Western professional militaries that they faced, they rapidly became adaptive—creating gray-zone tactics that suited their gray-zone environment. To fail in this task meant a quick death.

The difficulty of the environment, combined with the superior power of their enemy, meant that the insurgents were under tremendous pressure to adapt. The speed of this adaptation was what was giving them the advantage. It wasn't how big you were; it was how quickly you adapted to the changing environment.

KEY IDEA: *Limitation drives adaptation. Let the ground grow you.*

As the pandemic first hit, many shaped by Taylorist thinking struggled. As lockdowns prevented in-person Sunday services, they feared their ability to lead their congregations would dissipate. However, my former pastor and friend Alan Hirsch saw things differently.

Alan reflected that one of the best ways to become better at chess was to play without a queen.[13] The queen is the most powerful piece. Thus the novice player can become overly dependent on the ability of the queen. With the queen gone, the player must learn to play the other pieces. Removing the queen forces a player to adapt and learn. Through this deliberate handicapping, the player becomes a more rounded and adaptive chess strategist, seeing possibilities that were not visible when the queen was on the board.

Alan noted that the Sunday service is the queen for the pastor, a powerful tool that we can become overly dependent on, which can, in turn, reduce our imaginations of what ministry and church can look like. With the arrival of the pandemic and the inability to meet in person came an opportunity. The queen was off the board. Some pastors fell into despair and frustration. Others held their breath until they could regather. Some imagined the moment as persecution and conspiracy. Alan, however, doesn't think like a Taylorist and is deeply attuned to the dynamics of complex systems after years of studying networks. What Alan was doing for pastors was reframing the moment as an opportunity. A chance to let the pressure push us into adaptation, to seed creativity in a moment of challenge.

The Taylorist finds a best practice and repeats it ad nauseam, hoping for success every time. The adaptive leader continually grows and looks for a change in the environment and goes prospecting for hidden sources of power to mine. David Kilcullen defines adaptation as the trait "that enables an entity to better and serve and reproduce itself; it is also the process of change, in response to environmental pressure, that gives rise to new traits."[14] This learning is vital for us to grasp. If we can learn to adapt, we create a dynamic of continual growth. When we face a demanding environment, let the difficulty grow you.

The adaptive leader continually grows and looks for a change in the environment and goes prospecting for hidden sources of power to mine.

Growth, however can only occur when there is the right amount of stress. "Too little stress leads to under-stimulation with no potential for positive adaptation, and too much stress will overwhelm the individual and leave them broken,"[15] notes Australian author and former special forces commander Ben Pronk. Yet this raises a question: What happens when we face pressure that feels as though it will break us? Secular specialists in adaptation and resilience like Pronk advocate finding the zone of just the right amount of stress that drives adaptation. Yet at this point, we can fall into an error of striving for resilience in our own strength. To become genuinely adaptive and resilient leaders within our gray zone moment, we must learn a different way, rooted in dependency on God. How to do this is where we turn next.

RECAP: THREE KEY TAKEAWAYS

- We have moved from a complicated world to a complex world.

- Complicated environments require efficiency. Complex environments require adaptability.

- Limitation drives adaptation. Let the ground grow you.

CHAPTER 11

The Anxious Frontier

The root of our anxiety is our disconnection from God; this means we cannot be a non-anxious presence without God's presence. To do so is simply a project of human striving, which attempts to solve anxiety in the world but only adds to it. The good news is that the Bible shows us that the wilderness is the place where we encounter and are refreshed by the presence of God. The wilderness is where non-anxious leaders are formed, where we learn to become adaptive, creative, and resilient leaders in God's strength, not ours.

FRIEDMAN'S ANXIETY

As I have reflected on Friedman's leadership model of a non-anxious presence, I marvel at the prescience of his analysis of contemporary society. Many experts accurately chart the technological or sociological direction of society. However, Friedman's description of the emotional direction of our society, written in the 1990s, is quite remarkable. I believe that his insights into anxiety and leadership and the posture of leadership as non-anxious are beneficial.

However, as I have reflected on his insights and put them into practice as a leader, there is one weakness in Friedman's diagnosis and solution that bothered me, and I struggled to put my finger on it for years. Then one day, it struck me. Friedman, who had spent so much time analyzing the anxiety of others, seemed to have his own anxiety.

I want to be fair to Friedman and not mischaracterize his work. Sadly he passed away before he could complete *A Failure of Nerve*. The book that we have today was edited and compiled by his family and friends into its final form. So my comments are taken with caution, fully aware that Friedman's thoughts as we have them in *A Failure of Nerve* may be incomplete.

Reading Friedman, I resonate with much of his analysis and solution. However, it has always bugged me that it can appear as though a kind of superhuman resilience is required to be impervious to the emotional pushback, disruption, and sabotage that leaders face. Friedman is proposing that leaders must lead from a non-anxious posture—that part I agree with. Yet adopting and maintaining a non-anxious presence in the face of systemic anxiety, pushback, betrayal, and emotional sabotage requires tremendous stamina, pain tolerance, and emotional discipline. How does one find such resources to lead? What power source do we plug into to adopt the non-anxious presence?

Friedman offers us some historical examples of what non-anxious leaders look like. He reveals how he envisions such leaders finding the resources to achieve such stamina and pain tolerance. When imagining what a non-anxious leader may look like, most of us probably imagine someone who manages to maintain a kind of outer and inner serenity in the face of pushback; however, what Friedman offers as a model of non-anxious leadership is the great explorers that discovered the New World.

Explorers possessed a rugged individualism, which drove them to leave the safety of the shore behind to discover new lands. Friedman focuses on Christopher Columbus as his example of a non-anxious leader who was able to set out in the spirit of adventure, and as a result, spark the birth of a new civilization in the "New World" of the Americas. As I read these examples, my enthusiasm begins to wane. Those presented by Friedman as exemplars of non-anxious leaders, while at times showing courage and adventurism, also had murderous track records, alongside imperialistic goals of colonization, which hardly qualify them as praiseworthy examples.

The model of a non-anxious leadership is essential in our time of viral anxiety and networked life. Yet what is suggested by Friedman as a final embodiment of a non-anxious leader seems to be the ideology of the American century, which championed radical and rugged individualism. Friedman appears beset by his own anxiety. Peppered throughout *A Failure of Nerve* is the gnawing fear that America is in a dangerous decline. The golden period—characterized by risk-taking individualism, adventurous exploration, and conquest of the wild—has passed. A new wild in the form of infectious human anxiety limited the freedom of leaders to break new ground.

THE FRONTIER

The myth of the frontier served several purposes. Firstly, it distracted from the repossession of First Nations land, as well as obscured the human cost of slavery and ongoing discrimination against African Americans. Secondly, the myth of the frontier, in the words of historian Richard Slotkin, reimagined the American West as "a mythic region whose wildness made it at once a region of darkness and an earthly paradise, a goad to civilization and a barrier to it; whose hidden magic was to be tapped only by self-reliant individualists."[1] It offered the faceless factory worker, or office bureaucrat of the Industrial Age, a cultural repository of romanticized figures—from cowboys to maverick gold hunters and rugged frontiersmen. Archetypes became the staple heroic figures of the silver screen and popular fiction. These figures sustained the ideology of the radical individual against the collective structures of the Industrial Age, which negated individualism. These frontier leadership archetypes have shaped our mental models of what leaders look and act like.

As the Western frontier closed, other frontiers were imagined. As America strode into the role of a world superpower, President John F. Kennedy proclaimed a "New Frontier" of progressive social policy and scientific evolution. Captain James T. Kirk, the lead character of *Star Trek*, played by William Shatner, captured the mood of the space race as a new environment for the rugged individual, proclaiming space "The Final Frontier." As the idealism of the sixties and the drive for social change ran aground, a new frontier was proclaimed by former radical Jerry Rubin, who gave up on a social revolution and instead looked to the "inner revolution of the seventies."[2] The new frontier was found in the inner space and life of the individual, which would be explored by various therapies, sexual experimentation, and spiritual adventurism. Yet despite the drive to push toward these new frontiers, the problem remained.

As individuals—formed with the values and ideology of individualism, freedom, and self-expression—we live in a world where we are subject to large-scale forces beyond our control. This tension gives rise to what academic Timothy Melley labels "agency panic," which he defines as an "intense anxiety about an apparent loss of autonomy, the conviction that one's actions are being controlled by someone else or that one has been 'constructed' by powerful, external agents."[3] This fear of a loss of autonomy drives much of contemporary culture's anxiety. We can sense some of this agency panic in Friedman's work, flowing into his vision of what healthy leadership looked like.

> **KEY IDEA:** *The American century offered the frontier myth of leadership, in which a heroic leader finds themselves by conquering the wilderness in their own strength.*

The great fear of the frontier myth is that the American spirit of leadership has been domesticated. The wilderness is then reimagined as a place in which the individual, stifled by the collectivist impulse of the city and state, may again rediscover the inner reserves of fortitude and throw off the shackles of domestication, becoming a world-changing leader. This myth, like the frontier itself, has pushed past the physical landmass of the United States, becoming America's "greatest gift to the imagination of the world."[4]

The frontier myth has been reinvented, moving past the archetypes of the cowboy, the explorer, and the frontiersman to contemporary incarnations such as the entrepreneur, the social media influencer, the maverick CEO, and the activist. These individuals escape the wilderness of hiddenness, obscurity, and ordinary life into a visible, almost transcendent, known-ness. This frontier framework of leadership, remixed and refreshed in our day, bleeds into contemporary Christian conceptions of leadership and warps our understanding of what it is to give one's life for the cause of Christ.

MURRAY'S FAILURE OF NERVE

Friedman begins his book with a quote from the Australian-born historian Gilbert Murray's book *The Five Stages of Greek Religion*. Murray was one of the founders of the secular humanist movement in the United Kingdom. He was shaped by the nineteenth-century idea that the world would move toward a brighter future through human power. Humanists believed that the great "failure of nerve" occurred in the ancient world, in which the heights of early Greek thought were replaced by

> an atmosphere in which the aim of the good man is not so much to live justly, to help the society to which he belongs and enjoy the esteem of his fellow creatures; but rather, by means of a burning faith, by contempt for the world and its standards, by ecstasy, suffering, and martyrdom, to be granted pardon for his unspeakable unworthiness, his immeasurable sins. There is an intensifying of certain spiritual emotions; an increase of sensitiveness, a failure of nerve.[5]

As this quote reveals, for Murray, a failure was more than just a leader succumbing to the anxiety and emotional landscape of their day. A failure of nerve was a return to faith. A realization of one's sinfulness and a desire to again be united with God. In Murray's estimation, this halted the progress of the great human project.

THE GOOD PAGAN'S FAILURE

Murray's concept of the "failure of nerve" reflects the emerging secularist stream of thought that had captured much of the British upper classes of the nineteenth century—offering its elites a justification for their imperial project, which was viewed as the mission to introduce Western civilization to those in foreign lands who were regarded as being mired in superstitions. Such an imperial vision created its mythic heroes. Rugged individuals conquered the far-flung frontiers of the empire and ruled the colonial outposts with verve. However, Rosalind, Murray's daughter, saw through it all. Rejecting the aristocratic humanist environment she was born into, she had her own "failure of nerve" and converted to Christianity.

On the eve of World War II, Rosalind Murray would write a book critiquing her father's thoughts, pointedly entitled *The Good Pagan's Failure.* Intriguingly, her cultural critique would contain many similarities with Edwin Friedman. However, Rosalind, writing several decades before Friedman, would claim that the West lives "under the rule of the crowd," where "it is crowd opinion which forms the ideas of the modern world."[6] Like Friedman, Rosalind feared the undifferentiated mass and saw anxiety sweeping the modern world. However, her diagnosis contains a vital addition.

Rosalind saw the "failure of the good pagan," embodied in the failing project of the well-intentioned elites of all political stripes who attempted to improve the world without God. Elites who looked down on what they saw as the undifferentiated masses, swept up in irrationality and emotions. Elites who desired from their positions of privilege to heal the ailments of the masses.

Rosalind saw that the project of the West was marked by the "good pagan," who wished to move history forward to perfect society but without any sense of their need for redemption. In Rosalind's estimation, the modern individual and the modern world refused to acknowledge their sinfulness. The absolute failure of nerve is when we recoil from the idea of fallenness—our impotence to improve the world without God and our need for redemption through the person of Christ.

> **KEY IDEA:** *Humans are fallen. Leaders cannot be saved by the frontier. We can only be saved by Christ. All our leadership must flow from this truth.*

Without this vital component of grasping our need for redemption and reconnection to God, the great danger is our drive to differentiate ourselves from the anxious reactive systems of our day. We fall back into independency rather than self-differentiation. What is independency? It is a helpful term used by Donald Mostrom, who uses it to delineate from the term *independence*, noting that independence can be positive when it is freedom of unhealthy dependence on others. Independency is harmful, according to Mostrom. It emerges from "the human drive for personal sovereignty, the desire to be without accountability to any other person."[7]

Mostrom affirms the biblical belief that this drive for independency finds its roots in our rebellion in the garden. He argues that humans "came to love our freedom from God with a passion that we give to few other things."[8] It is this drive for freedom from God that is the true source of the relational anxiety that infects human relationships:

> We will not fully understand our problems in human relationships until we see them as the expression of the active rebellion and independency which has afflicted human nature. A vast arsenal of weapons against human fellowship grows out of this route. Fear, anger, jealousy, envy, bitterness, revenge, flattery, accusation, and many other injurious conditions develop from

the sickness of a human nature estranged from God and trying unsuccessfully to defend its own "god-status" against all comers.[9]

The seed of the anxiety that invades and infects human social systems is found in the disconnection from the presence of God, which occurred in the garden. This is the engine that powers both the toxic anxiety in our social systems, which worships conformity at the cost of growth, and independency, which worships at the altar of radical freedom.

In our disconnection from God, we rebel against responsibility, relationships, and life-giving rules. Thus, anxiety and independency live in a codependent relationship.

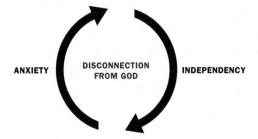

ANXIETY   DISCONNECTION FROM GOD   INDEPENDENCY

This explains the problem the contemporary self finds itself caught in. We want the freedom and autonomy of radical individualism while being dependent on the opinions and emotional climate of the crowd. This is the myth of the frontier, in which we yearn for the illusionary freedom of the wilderness, seeking salvation in it, rather than in the God who is found in the wilderness. We seek the comfort of the crowd's consensus but find ourselves spiritually stagnant on the couch with our heads buried in our phones.

In our disconnection from God, we rebel against responsibility, relationships, and life-giving rules.

Mostrom rightly contends that for health and emotional healing to return to the world of human relationships, the infectious foe of anxiety must be vanquished. We need something more than mere community-improved social connection, or even religiously tinged "fellowship." Donald G. Mostrom writes:

> Rather we are talking about the profound effects of God's presence with his people. We are talking about an intimate connection with God, a basic healing of life that comes about increasingly as the negative dynamics of independency are overcome and the healing presence of the Spirit of God is at work in us and our human relationships as well. This is really what Christianity is about.[10]

Our human systems will only heal when we are reconnected with God. We can only move toward a better future as we recognize our sinfulness and need for Christ's saving work on the cross, reconnecting us to God.

KEY IDEA: *We can only be non-anxious presences with God's presence.*

This reconnection to God, His Word, and revelation enables the leader to be correctly orientated in the world, recalibrating our leadership to heaven's pattern.

RECAP: THREE KEY TAKEAWAYS

- The American century offered the frontier myth of leader-ship, in which heroic leaders find themselves by conquering the wilderness in their own strength.

- Humans are fallen. Leaders cannot be saved by the frontier. We can only be saved by Christ. All our leadership must flow from this truth.

- We can only be non-anxious presences with God's presence.

CHAPTER 12

Gaining a Heavenly Orientation

As he faced the complex gray-zone dynamics of Iraq, General Stanley McCrystal turned to the ideas of John Boyd, a maverick strategist, both maligned and celebrated in equal measure. Boyd created the now-famous strategic tool—the OODA loop. OODA stands for *Observe, Orient, Decide,* and *Act.* Boyd, an Air Force pilot, like his peers was trained to fight in propellor aircraft. His instructors had learned their craft in the air battles of World War II. However, Boyd's baptism into battle occurred in the cockpit of a jet fighter, battling in the kill zone over Korea.

Whereas slower propeller-powered aircraft could enable pilots to observe their location, jet fighters moved at much faster speeds. This technological leap made them more powerful fighting machines. Yet it also meant that a pilot could become completely disoriented, believing that they were the right way up when in fact, they were upside down and careering toward the ground. The old strategic and linear formula allowed pilots to *observe* where the enemy was, *decide* how they would respond, and *act.* However, in the high speed, complex, and chaotic environment of jet fighter dogfighting, Boyd realized that a crucial element was missing: *orientation*, knowing where you are in relation to your environment.

One could observe, but if your observation was wrong, it meant your orientation was off. As a result, your decisions and actions would lead to disaster. In the commotion of high-speed battle, Boyd understood that chaotic environments were disorienting. Thus, in chaos, we need orientation. We need to know how the environment has changed and properly reorient ourselves to that changed environment before we can chart our direction of action.

KEY IDEA: *In a gray zone, proper orientation is essential.*

Boyd understood that to succeed in a rapidly changing environment, we needed to respond rapidly; this is why, in the words of Boyd's biographer Robert Coram, orientation "is the single most important part of the cycle."[1] The pilot or leader must have "a deep intuitive understanding of one's relationship to the rapidly changing environment."[2] Boyd saw his OODA loop as having a much broader application than just air battle. He noted that many leaders fail to succeed because they observe their environment and view challenges through faulty lenses, seeing what they want to see rather than the actual shape of the environment in which they operate and the obstacles they face.

Distilling Boyd's thought, Coram notes that "if our mental processes become . . . isolated from the unfolding, constantly dynamic outside world, we experience mismatches between our mental images and reality. Then confusion and discord and uncertainty not only result but continue to increase."[3] Proper orientation connects us with the reality of our environment rather than what we think our environment is.

Julia Galef calls this the *scout mindset*,[4] which she contrasts with the *soldier mindset*. The soldier appears on the battlefield already convinced of the battle they will fight. In contrast, the scout approaches the battlefield with an open mind. First, the scout observes the lay of the land from a distance. Then, before committing to action, they first orient themselves to the realities of the context and environment, gauging the strength and nature of their enemy.

REALITY VS. IDEOLOGY

Many leaders are ill-equipped to face our gray zone moment because we bring ideological baggage or we carry yesterday's strategies and are unwilling to see how the environment and context we face has rapidly changed. Orientation connects to the reality of our situation. Swedish diplomat Dag Hammarskjold reflected that "to have humility is to experience reality."[5] Being connected to the reality of the situation can lead us to realize our weaknesses, especially in the face of a complex challenge like our networked world and our gray zone moment. This mental shift can be challenging for leaders, surrounded by anxious followers who presume that they have all the answers while also demanding quick-fix solutions from their leaders. Such pressure can launch us forward into decisions and actions disconnected from orientation. The anxiety of the crowd clouds our observation. Orientation is required. Yet orientation requires humility, for when we understand our weakness, it enables us to trust fully in God's strength.

This is a good reminder. In this book, we have examined a lot of military strategies. While the Bible uses military strategy, it also subtly undermines it. In 1 Samuel 13–14, Israel, armed only with farming tools, defeats a superior Philistine force as God sends the enemy into a blind panic. The message is clear—with God, Israel is not to operate or fight as the world does. The eventual solution comes when God sends King Jesus to show us the heavenly pattern of a king, and He initiates the kingdom of God, the heavenly pattern of a people.

KEY IDEA: *In a gray zone, proper orientation can only come from a heavenly perspective.*

In comparison to this heavenly pattern, human thought falls short. The military theorists in this chapter have provided some excellent analysis of the networked gray zone, helping us unthink some of our Taylorist approaches to leadership. However, followed to their logical extension, they can be unsatisfying or even profoundly troubling. Taken to its extreme, Boyd's OODA loop can create a leader who operates as a kind of autonomous military drone. Both Galef and Boyd end up collapsing back to the myth of the radical individual, operating their agenda effectively in their environment. Although brilliant, they offer us another take on the individualist ideology of the American century. They both return to human power as the solution.

The result of McChrystal's analysis leads the general to offer a solution that may be helpful but ultimately underwhelming. To be more adaptive, McChrystal encourages more connection and communication to facilitate greater coordination. In his hierarchical military context where bureaucratic silos can form, he created a kind of giant weekly team meeting, which he called the "Team of Teams," where the leadership under his command could share

innovations, report, and engage in team learning. Potentially helpful, yes, but underwhelming in the face of the gray zone challenge
he previously so eloquently described. However, in each of these
approaches, there is a kernel of truth.

> **GALEF'S SCOUT MINDSET:** Humbly approach and con-
> nect with the reality of your situation.
>
> **BOYD'S OODA LOOP:** Orient to your environment and
> context correctly.
>
> **MCCRYSTAL'S TEAM OF TEAMS:** Communication is
> the key to adaptability.

In the Bible, King David's strategic approach combines each of
these elements but reorients them heavenward. As a result, it offers
a far more satisfying and biblical way forward.

HEAVEN IS THE ORIENTATION

As we have learned, orientation is essential. David's humility enabled him to understand the earthly context in which he operated.
Yet vitally, he was also oriented to the heavenly reality. In the years
before David's anointing as king, we are told that "in those days the
word of the LORD was rare; there were not many visions" (1 Sam. 3:1).
This lack of spiritual vision hampers the ability of those in charge
of Israel to lead properly. Eli the priest, who leads Israel, has failing
eyesight, yet he cannot detect the heavenly signal in his midst. This
is ultimately what much of human leadership is—a reading of the
earthly environment and a strategy to operate effectively within it.

Samuel detects the heavenly signal—the voice of God. At first, he is confused, unable to distinguish the divine and human voice. However, this is part of his preparation. God is laying the foundations of the renewal to come through teaching Samuel what my friend Terry Walling calls *voice recognition*. That is the ability of leaders to hear the voice of God, His Word and His Spirit, amid the hubbub of the world. Only through voice recognition can we begin to orient ourselves correctly in the world in which He called us to lead and minister. This leads us to an important principle: *detection precedes direction*.

To partner with God as He brings renewal in the world, in the systems and organizations where we live and lead, we must learn to detect His voice before moving forward.

Before Samuel could gain direction from God's voice, he first had to learn to hear God's voice; this is the missing component for many leaders. We are awash in rich resources on how to lead. Yet much of it, even some Christian works, emerges from an observation only attuned to the earthly environment. The secular approach to leadership refuses to acknowledge or tune into the heavenly signal of God's voice.

Taylorism may show us the most effective path from A to B. However, it cannot show us if the path is the right path. To partner with God as He brings renewal in the world, in the systems and organizations where we live and lead, we must learn to detect His voice before moving forward; this is a countercultural act in an anxious system, which demands instant action, quick fixes, and fast-acting remedies for pain. Waiting on the Lord, seeking His voice, is an act of revolutionary stillness. This leads us to another critical principle: *detection leads to differentiation*.

Samuel at first mistook the voice of God for Eli's voice. As he learned to detect the voice of God, he had to learn to differentiate the voice of humans from the voice of God. Voice recognition is a crucial leadership skill because we must learn to distinguish the voice of God from the inevitable anxious voice of the crowd that the leader encounters as they emerge into their leadership. This is vital as we increasingly move into our gray zone moment when our networked world offers countless feedback loops to insert human voices and opinions into our consciousness. Detection and differentiation become easier as we learn to walk in intimacy with God.

God calling Samuel was akin to a phone call to recommence a relationship after a long absence. Samuel heard the voice of God. David walked with God in the wilderness. David's leadership developed a deep intimacy with his heavenly Father. David's ability to detect God's voice, to differentiate God's voice from the voice of the crowd, flowed from his intimacy with God's presence. This leads us to another fundamental principle:

KEY IDEA: *God's presence turns an unformed wilderness into a garden of holy growth.*

At the beginning of Genesis, we encounter the world in the moments before creation. It is mere earth. A desert devoid of growth and life. The waters represent the world's primal chaos, wild and unformed, waiting to be brought into its heavenly order. "Hovering over the face of the waters in the beginning," Meredith Kline remarks, was the Spirit, "the Creator-King present in almighty power, poised to fashion deep-and-darkness into a heaven on earth."[6] The earth is still unformed, the chaos still disordered, yet the hovering Spirit is a sign and promise of the future growth potential of the formless earth. Kline notes that "we behold in the Spirit-Presence hovering over the world at its beginning the shape of the world to come."[7]

What does this mean? The Bible tells us that at the beginning of the world God created the heavens and the earth. So we get the idea of the creation of the earth, but most of us miss the fact that God also created the heavens at creation. The recognition of this fact leads us to ponder the nature of the heavens.

In describing the earthly temple, the writer of Hebrews informs the reader that the Jerusalem priesthood "serve[s] at a sanctuary that is a copy and shadow of what is in heaven. This is why Moses was warned when he was about to build the tabernacle: 'See to it that you make everything according to the pattern shown you on the mountain'" (Heb. 8:5). For everything on earth, there is a heavenly pattern. Biblical scholar James Jordan writes that "heaven forms the model for the earth—socially, morally, spiritually, and in every other way."[8] What we see at creation is the Spirit coming to mediate the heavenly pattern upon the unformed wildness of the world. The "Spirit proceeded from heaven," Jordan explains, and "brought a blueprint with Him, and began the work of shaping the world after the heavenly model."[9]

God's word, spoken at creation, transformed the chaos into the imprint of heaven upon earth. This is why Jesus teaches His disciples to pray, "Our Father in heaven, hallowed be your name, your kingdom come, your will be done, on earth as it is in heaven" (Matt. 6:9–10). Heaven is where God's will happens in fullness. Thus the presence of God comes to show us how the wilderness can be reformed according to God's design. The word is the seed that transforms the wilderness sin into an Eden, birthing new creation.

We are getting closer to understanding why heaven is our ultimate orientation. Over every wilderness, chaotic environment, and gray zone, the Spirit hovers. The presence of God is always present, offering us the pattern of heaven. The plans, the heavenly blueprints that signal the renewal of any moment, and the reordering of the most chaotic environments. Every moment, every action, every thought, every problem contains the renewal potential of remaking that moment according to the pattern of heaven. This is hope.

You were made in the image of God to bring chaos into order, as you act as a channel of God's will on earth.

God's word spoke the earth into a divine order, which reflected the heavenly pattern. God then creates man and woman in His image. Humans, like creation, also are marked by the pattern of heaven, reflecting the image of God. As God creates and brings heaven's imprint upon the wild earth's unformed chaos, so too will humans. Jordan writes of humanity's purpose:

> Man is to labor to take the raw materials of the earth and remodel it according to the heavenly blueprint. . . . This explains to us why God would initially create two environments, rather than just one. Man was created to act as God's agent, His son, in the world. Man was going to be given the delightful task of transfiguring the world from glory to glory according to the heavenly model.[10]

Now we are cooking with gas. You are not created to remain paralyzed in anxiety. You were not created to offer an anxious crowd quick-fix solutions and a panacea for their lostness. You were not patterned after heaven to retreat into a comfort zone. You were made in the image of God to bring chaos into order, as you act as a channel of God's will on earth. The Spirit manifests the pattern of heaven in the world, and we mediate that pattern as God's workers in creation.

The kingdom breaking out is when the heavenly pattern is initiated on earth. That is where you are called to be, at the point where heaven kisses the earth. At that intersection, the ways of the kingdom are revealed. We access a different power source to lead from.

RECAP: THREE KEY TAKEAWAYS

- In a gray zone, proper orientation is essential.

- In a gray zone, proper orientation can only come from the heavenly perspective.

- God's presence turns an unformed wilderness into a garden of holy growth.

CHAPTER 13

Hidden Kingdom
Power Laws

You may have heard of what is known popularly as the Butterfly Effect. A butterfly flaps its wings on one side of the world and creates a hurricane on the other side of the planet. You also may have heard of the 80/20 rule in which 80 percent of our productivity is generated by 20 percent of our effort. Both of these are popular expressions of the power laws that operate in our complex world. Power laws describe how small inputs can have disproportionate effects in complex systems.

A linear system will show a proportionate response. For example, a golfer hitting a ball will expect the ball to travel a distance proportional to their strength and skill in striking the ball. After hitting a ball with all their might, the golfer will not expect the ball only to move an inch, nor will they expect the ball to travel several thousand miles. However, in a complex world, small things can have a significant impact.

Last week I purchased a new car on my phone, something I would never do in normal times. Why? Well, my new Toyota Camry will not arrive in Melbourne for approximately four more months. This delay is occurring worldwide in the global supply chain because of a series of small inputs that have thrown the whole system out. A COVID outbreak in a factory in southern China that makes computer conductors for cars means that I have to wait four months to get my new car. Complex environments are unpredictable and nonlinear because they contain what are known as different power laws. Why is this?

KEY IDEA: *In a complex world, small things can have a significant impact.*

In linear systems, there is a hierarchy of cause and effect; however, in the nonlinear dynamics of complex systems, small players can have disproportionate impacts, and large forces can find themselves quickly overwhelmed. The power laws and nonlinear dynamics mean that tipping points can be reached where a small input or change within the complex system can quickly multiply and hit a tipping point. The initially small input or change becomes a full-blown phenomenon within the system. The power of multiplication can take off rapidly in complex systems, with surprising results. Using an epidemiological term that has become part of popular culture, things can "go viral" in a complex system.

There are power laws that are active within the kingdom of God. Oriented to heaven's pattern, the apostle Paul writes, "For when I am weak, then I am strong" (2 Cor. 12:10). Paul was a tiny input within the complex system known as the Greco-Roman world. However, his impact was gigantic. Paul was a walking example of a kingdom power law, writing, "Therefore I will boast all the more gladly about my weaknesses, so that Christ's power may rest on me" (2 Cor. 12:9). The armies of Rome were no match for a tiny man who was a leader oriented to God.

KEY IDEA: *The kingdom of God operates according to its own power laws. With God, the weak are strong.*

In the most complex and challenging environments, we can uncover hidden power when we are oriented to heaven.

GOLIATH

David was in an unusual position. The prophet Samuel had anointed him to be king, yet another sat on the throne. He had a promise but no position. So instead, he moved between the royal court of Israel, where he served the increasingly troubled King Saul, and the flock of sheep he tended in the wilderness.

The big news story of the day was the amassing of the Philistine military forces and their threats to Israel's security. Israel had previously routed the Philistines, as they relied not on weapons but the strength of the Lord. However, now anxiety pulsed through the troops of Israel as the rules of the game changed. Facing the troops was Goliath, a behemoth warrior. Goliath's taunts turned faith into fear. Saul, the warrior king, is overtaken by terror and is paralyzed. The army of Israel reaches an impasse, devoid of strategy and strength.

David's older brothers are warriors and were sent to the battlefront. However, although anointed by his heavenly Father, David is still not appreciated by his earthly father. He continues to fulfill his role as the family shepherd, sent into the wild places. Finally, Jesse, David's father, orders him to travel to the front lines of Israel's war with the Philistines to deliver food to his brothers.

If the ancient context obscures the irony of this scene, let me put it in modern terms. The soon-to-be king of Israel, anointed by God to lead His nation, to build the house of God, is relegated to the role of the skinny Uber Eats kid on an electric scooter.

To make matters worse, upon arrival at the battlefield, his brothers, enduring the taunts of Goliath, vent their frustrations at their younger sibling. They mock his role as shepherd and his life in the wilderness. They attack the very thing that sets David apart, his heart after God, accusing him of having an arrogant heart. They claim that David, who will become Israel's great strategist, is merely here to spectate the battle from the sidelines. His brothers make clear to him the line between soldier and civilian.

If there is one institution that defines the idea of centralized power, it is the military. Armies are top-down, hierarchical organizations that run by the book. As they grow in strength and size, militaries spawn massive bureaucracies and generate iron-clad standard operating procedures. They are effective at executing tasks and the repetition of best practices yet often struggle to innovate when change comes, and the contours of the battlefield may take on new and unseen forms.

For Israel's army, Goliath's appearance had changed the battlefield, leaving them bereft of solutions to this shift in the power balance. David, coming not from the central hierarchy of the military forces but rather a civilian from the peripheries, suggests a different way forward. David is brought before King Saul, who points out his youth and inexperience. David, however, doesn't waver, replying, "Your servant has been keeping his father's sheep. When a lion or a bear came and carried off a sheep from the flock, I went after it, struck it and rescued the sheep from its mouth."[1]

We mustn't view this statement through our contemporary lens and romanticized view of nature. The royal court, the military leaders, and those listening would not have been impressed by David's statement. Only those on the lower rungs of the social hierarchy dwelt in the wilderness and dealt with animals, especially predators. Shepherds were at the bottom of the social ladder.

Despite the resistance of his audience David continues, adding, "The LORD who rescued me from the paw of the lion and the paw of the bear will rescue me from the hand of this Philistine" (1 Sam. 17:37). Saul sends David on his way, offering him the military uniform of the king, which David refuses since the armor does not fit. This action is filled with symbolism. David cannot win this battle with someone else's mantle and with yesterday's tools.

Instead, David heads away from the royal court to the stream. Redolent of the streams of quiet waters, David was led by his Lord in the wilderness, taking what seems like a paltry arsenal of smooth rocks for battling the champion of the Philistines. David confronts Goliath, defeating him with an innovative approach rooted in his trust in God. David proclaims, "Is it not by sword or spear that the LORD saves; for the battle is the LORD's, and he will give all of you into our hands" (1 Sam. 17:47). David flips the script and wins with the most creative and unusual of tactics. How did this happen?

UNCOVERING HIDDEN POWER

Professor of management Richard Rumelt lauds David's strategy, noting that the defeat of Goliath "teaches us that our preconceived ideas of strength and weakness may be unsound." Rumelt notes that what David possessed was a "decisive asymmetry." In other words, David uncovered a power imbalance that no one else saw. Rumelt notes that a decisive asymmetry rests on "how someone can see what others have not, or what they have ignored, and thereby discover a pivotal objective and create an advantage."[2] David's marginal position, his distance from the center of power, was viewed by the army, Saul, and even his brothers as a disadvantage. Yet it offered him a different vantage point with which to approach this challenge. David, in his earthly weakness, held a decisive asymmetry.

David won the battle by applying the lessons learned in the wilderness. Before David had even approached the Philistine front, the battle was already won. Where? In the quiet spaces of the wilderness. In hiddenness. In the growth that can only occur off the radar. Richard Rumelt argues that good strategy "uncovers the hidden power in situations."[3] This is what David did. He knew that God was his strength. The Lord was his stronghold, his most decisive asymmetrical advantage. David's battlefield orientation was not set with earthly eyes but with spiritual vision. This perspective opened new possibilities and innovative approaches to confront a changing landscape and adapt to evolving challenges and threats.

KEY IDEA: *The experience of leading in the wilderness offers us lessons in kingdom power laws.*

As we face a complex world, growing in its levels of complexity at a rapid rate that throws us into the wilderness, we need to reframe this wilderness, this challenge, as a school of innovation through which God seeds the next season of kingdom ground to be taken. The kingdom of God is filled with asymmetrical advantages. Let us continue to learn from David, as his life illustrates the way in the wilderness and the leadership lessons of a shepherd.

RECAP: THREE KEY TAKEAWAYS

- In a complex world, small things can have a significant impact.

- The kingdom of God operates according to its own power laws. With God the weak are strong.

- The experience of leading in the wilderness offers us lessons in kingdom power laws.

CHAPTER 14

Pressure and the Presence

King David faced betrayal, emotional sabotage, and a rebellion by his loved ones. He led in an anxious environment undergoing tremendous cultural change. Yet David is recognized by Scripture as one of the most outstanding leaders the world has ever seen. David wasn't king because he possessed deep natural reserves of grit and stamina. David was a non-anxious presence because he had the presence of God.

David offers us a model of what a non-anxious presence founded by the presence of God looks like. When we first encounter David, he appears to be an afterthought. Seeking to anoint a new king, Samuel seeks out Jesse. Jesse's son Eliab seems to be perfect leadership material. Yet God reminds the prophet to look not at the outward attributes but rather at the heart. As Samuel passes Jesse's sons, now viewing them with a spiritual rather than earthly lens, none are suitable. Finally, Jesse remarks that he has another son, who is out tending the sheep. This seemingly innocuous statement is, in reality, deeply profound. David is out in the wild.

David is not in the wilderness taking ground. Nor is he trying to find himself as he expands the frontiers of civilization in a heroic quest. David is not an explorer. David is a shepherd. In the shepherd, we find a biblical model of leadership, of a non-anxious presence, which is not dependent on reserves of personal power but on the presence of God—encountered in the wild places.

David the shepherd, the man after God's heart, like the people of God, is formed in the wilderness. This is not the wilderness of the American frontier. Instead, in the Hebrew imagination, the wilderness was not a place to be conquered but rather a place of challenge and confrontation. A gray zone outside of protective walls, both physical and relational.

In the shepherd, we find a biblical model of leadership, of a non-anxious presence, which is not dependent on reserves of personal power but on the presence of God—encountered in the wild places.

The ancient Hebrews were not individualists. To be away from family and kin was a terrifying prospect in terms of one's vulnerability to attack and the elements but also in terms of one's identity. In tribal societies, one's entire sense of self comes from those you are in a relationship with. You are your people. They are the marker, which informs you of who you are, what your role is, and where you belong.

Thus, David's duties in the wilderness illuminate us to his place in his family and offer us an insight into how he must have felt about his place in the world. He was overlooked and forgotten. David endured not just the wilderness in which he was physically isolated. He was also emotionally and relationally isolated. When Samuel comes to anoint one of Jesse's sons for kingship, Jesse doesn't believe that there is any potential for greatness within his David. He is the runt of the family—an afterthought.

Yet there is something special about David that earthly eyes cannot register. Alan Redpath notes that "the public anointing was the outcome of what had taken place in private between David and God long before."[1] Before the moment of his anointing, which was played out in front of others, David had encountered God. Redpath wonders when this moment was, speculating, "Perhaps David met with God one night under the stars as he saw the heavens declaring the glory of God and the earth showing forth His handiwork. Perhaps the young shepherd drew near to the heart of God as he watched his flock on the mountainside."[2]

The where, when, and how don't matter to us; they remain sealed in the precious hidden moments between God and David. What matters is the fruit we see. That is the evidence of a life that had encountered the presence of God in the wilderness. His isolation, although undoubtedly painful, distanced him from others yet brought him close to God.

David's psalms are filled with the imagery of the wilderness and the closeness of God in such places. The Twenty-Third Psalm is filled with the images of the life of a shepherd, isolated from human connection and community, vulnerable, distanced from the dependence on the tribal dwelling places and human strongholds, yet who walks closely with God, dependent on Him for everything.

David was not the archetype of the heroic explorer conquering wildlands; instead, in the wild, God conquered his heart. David the shepherd, placed in the wilderness, finds God. The explorer heads into the wilderness to find glory. The shepherd of God is humbled by the wilderness to be shaped by God and thus elevates Him through worship.

THE WILDERNESS GIVES US DISTANCE, DIFFERENTIATING US

Without God's presence, the wilderness offers only isolation. With the presence of God, the wilderness offers us insulation from the deception of the crowd. Henri Nouwen, reflecting on how God uses deserts and wilderness experiences to shape us, wrote, "Our society is not a community radiant with the love of Christ, but a dangerous network of domination and manipulation in which we can easily get entangled and lose our soul."[3] Nouwen argued that our entanglement in this toxic social network warped our sense of self. "Secularity is a way of being dependent on the responses of our milieu."[4] This anxious secular self "points to the need for ongoing and increasing affirmation, Who am I? I am the one who is liked, praised, admired, disliked, hated or despised. Whether I am a pianist, a businessman or a minister, what matters is how I am perceived by my world."[5]

However, to rid us of our secular selves, Nouwen argued, we must embrace the experience of the wilderness. Without this wilderness, "we remain victims of our society and continue to be entangled in the illusions of the false self. Jesus himself entered into this furnace. There he was tempted with the three compulsions of the world: to be relevant ('turn stones into loaves'), to be spectacular ('throw yourself down'), and to be powerful ('I will give you all these kingdoms'). There he affirmed God as the only source of his identity ('You must worship the Lord your God and serve him alone')."[6] The wilderness thus detoxes us from our addiction to approval, which is a slippery slope to the creation of a secular self, formed to both please and appease the network. The wilderness does the work of differentiation for us.

Separate from the crowd's voice, in the wilderness, David found and was formed by the voice of God. In Psalm 4, David addresses the toxic crowd: "How long will you love delusions and seek false gods?" (Ps. 4:2). David can ask this and see through the idolatry and fantasy of his culture, having gained the perspective of distance from the mob. He is differentiated unto the Lord, recording the deep knowledge "that the LORD has set apart his faithful servant for himself" (Ps. 4:3).

With God, differentiation becomes more than the distance from the anxious crowd; it becomes a calling. A holy set-apartness. A return to the right order in which God is our primary connection, the foundational relationship of our life, around which all other relationships can be reordered.

DIFFERENTIATION LEADS TO DEPENDENCY

David's deep spiritual communion was forged in the isolation of the wilderness. Isolation became differentiation. Differentiation became dependency. Yet we also have the psalms, a behind-the-scenes account of the inner spiritual life of the king. Many of these psalms were written at various stages of life, reflecting the challenges he faced as king.

In David's psalms, the wilderness themes shine through, both in the imagery (streams, mountains, wild animals) and at a deeper level. David's faith was forged in the wilderness, on the peripheries, carrying that experience even as he was ensconced as king on the throne, at the very center of political power. The psalms speak of David's dependency on God. In Psalm 18, David proclaims the Lord is his strength, shield, rock, and stronghold. David is separate and vulnerable in the wilderness, yet this leads David to make God his strength. The wilderness teaches David to live in utter dependency on the Father, trusting Him to provide and offer sanctuary and protection.

THE WILDERNESS IS WHERE
WE ENCOUNTER HIS PRESENCE

Nouwen adds an essential extra layer. The wilderness, the gray zone, "is the place of the great struggle and the great encounter."[7] Corey Russell writes of the biblical wilderness that it is "throughout the Bible we see that God chooses again and again to form His people in the wilderness. It is the furnace of transformation. The place where our facades, illusions, fantasies, and props are removed and we come face-to-face with our nothingness. In the wilderness, God strips us of our independence and rebellion and teaches us to depend on Him."[8]

Humans have used furnaces throughout history to shape, transform, and re-create raw material. Furnaces contain fire. This is true of the furnace of transformation that is the wilderness. It is deep in the wilderness that Moses encounters the holy and inextinguishable fire of the burning bush, which contains the presence of God. The wilderness is where we encounter the fire and presence of God. God commands Moses, "Take off your sandals, for the place where you are standing is holy ground" (Ex. 3:5). The presence of God turns the hard ground into holy ground.

There was a divine purpose in David's vocation as a shepherd. The role of the shepherd is to lead and manage the welfare of sheep in the wilderness. The shepherd is both protector and guide, designated to protect sheep from the ravages of the wilderness. The environment of the wilderness and the role of the shepherd provided David with a kind of university education in dependency on God.

Phillip Keller, a farmer and shepherd from East Africa reflecting on Psalm 23, notes that "when all is said and done, the welfare of any flock is entirely dependent upon the management afforded them by their owner."[9] The sheep are utterly dependent upon their shepherd.

When David declares the Lord his shepherd, he is expressing his utter dependency on God. David declares that God the shepherd "makes [him] lie down in green pastures" (Ps. 23:2). With his insider knowledge, Keller informs us that it is rare for a sheep to lie down, that "owing to their timidity they refuse to lie down unless they are free of all fear."[10] Sheep are naturally anxious creatures. They are also a herd, animals taking their cues from the rest of the flock.

We use the term *sheeplike* as an insult to describe someone who does not think for themselves. Anxiety over a predator can send a flock into a panic. Anxiety also ripples through a flock when there is an imbalance in the social hierarchy of the flock as battles occur over who is the top sheep. "Because of the social behaviour within a flock sheep will not lie down unless they are free from friction with others of their kind."[11] As he learned the craft of shepherding, Keller came to understand that "nothing so quieted and reassured the sheep as to see me in the field. The presence of their master and owner and protector put them at ease as nothing else could do."[12]

The presence of the shepherd calms the anxiety of the flock, enabling them to lie down in green pastures. Keller adds, "In the Christian's life there is no substitute for the keen awareness that my Shepherd is nearby. There is nothing like Christ's presence to dispel the fear, the panic, the terror of the unknown."[13] The only presence that can calm our anxiety is the peace that transcends all understanding and flows from giving our whole life to Christ, as we depend on Him for everything.

KEY IDEA: *The presence of God turns the hard ground into holy ground.*

STRONGHOLDS ARE SANCTUARIES

Leadership in our anxious age, and indeed in any age, is a battle against anxiety and sabotage. As we have learned, these challenges can lead us to seek refuge in the world's strongholds. As we move into leadership, we can even seek refuge in the strongholds that we build. This is the great tension of human leadership.

One of the worst things that can happen to a leader is for them to have success before they have been humbled, broken, and prepared by the Lord.

Interestingly, Saul begins his kingship like David, still a man attuned to the wild. In 1 Samuel 11, we find King Saul returning from working the fields with his oxen. He is king but is not yet domesticated by the pomp and power of the palace, for he still works the land. Saul was a member of the tribe of Benjamin, the smallest tribe of Israel. The insignificance of his tribe caused Saul to be initially surprised when Samuel anointed him (see 1 Sam. 9:21). Perhaps this initial humility and connection to the wild are why we find Saul in the early days with the Spirit of God powerfully upon him.

Yet the story of Saul is a cautionary tale. It shows us that one of the worst things that can happen to a leader is for them to have success before they have been humbled, broken, and prepared by the Lord. When this happens, our success can quickly become our stronghold.

Most of us are happy to have the first part of Saul's story. We would be glad to emerge from the obscurity of the wilderness to be powerfully anointed by God, going on to be used by Him powerfully. In many ways, the first part of Saul's leadership journey mirrors the celebrity dream so prevalent in our society, the archetype of the person plucked from nowhere who becomes a star.

However, the story of Saul warns us of the dangers of early successes. Saul does not end well. Later on, the man who humbly wondered why God had chosen him to be king erected monuments to himself. His successes, his inflated sense of self, the myth that he had built up the kingdom in his own strength became strongholds that he retreated into—driving him mad with power, insecurity, and jealousy. The insecure leader can rapidly turn into an arrogant leader as they find solace, identity, and direction in the flattery of others. The voice of the crowd then drowns out the still small voice of God encountered in the wilderness.

Saul fell for what psychologist John O'Neil labels "mythic success—a potent elixir compounded of wealth, power, privilege, and freedom from care."[14] Mythic success occurs when we start buying our own press. It happens when we are seduced by the crowd, molding ourselves to be the mythic answer to their anxiety. Swooning at the mob's attention, we reach beyond our natural talents and limits of what we are called to do. We become entitled, expecting a payoff for our Christian service, sabotaged by our definitions of success. This is what happened to Saul—he made his success his stronghold, and it ruined him. God protected David from success coming too early. He did this by sending him into the school of the wilderness.

THE SCHOOL OF THE WILDERNESS

One of the significant differences between King Saul and King David is that David returned to the wilderness. God had deeply prepared David in the wilderness. It was to this preparation in the wilderness that David would return, even when comfortably ensconced in the palace. When David was not physically present in the wilderness, the seed of growth initiated within David in the wild continued to grow in him. David recognized that the wilderness was a teacher. Its greatest lesson we must never forget is that no human construction can ever replace God as our stronghold.

KEY IDEA: *In the wilderness, David learned that God was his ultimate stronghold.*

Saul, from his stronghold of success and self-reliance, would send David back into the wilderness. Saul had the capital and the throne. David had the anointing. Yet even with this anointing, God sends David back into the wilderness. Why? R. T. Kendall offers us a vital insight into the way that God forms us through moments of wilderness and pressure:

> David wasn't ready to be King. God might have taken Saul away in his wrath then and there rather than wait for years and years. God had a different idea for David—that Saul be the means of David's sanctification! David wasn't ready to be King. He had a powerful anointing, yes. But he needed to be honed and refined. In the years to come, that anointing in David was to increase and develop so that when his time had truly come, David would be a transformed servant of the Holy Spirit.[15]

We are sent into the wilderness, often repeatedly, to face the pressure that refines.

We must understand God uses pressure to grow us during this gray zone moment of wilderness, filled with so many challenges.

For David, R. T. Kendall notes that "suffering was David's passport to a greater anointing."[16] Pressure creates diamonds. The word *diamond* comes from the Greek *adamas*, which means unconquerable or invincible.

In hiddenness, in the most silent of sufferings, diamonds are created. . . . diamonds are made pure by intense pressure. So too are we. No pressure, no holiness.

There is something about diamonds, this rugged, translucent stone that has captured humanity's imagination. Diamonds initially don't start as diamonds. They begin as simple carbon, something very ordinary. But this carbon is transformed from a common substance into something rare, incredible, and near invincible. How? Through pressure.

PRESSURE CREATES DIAMONDS

We have already learned about the incredible power that resides deep in the earth and is released during volcanic eruptions like an explosion of Krakatoa. It is this moment of tremendous pressure that creates a diamond. Diamonds begin their process of transformation hundreds of miles under the earth's crust. They are made in hiddenness. When stress comes, pressure often meets us in a kind of hiddenness. Pain and pressure are isolating. This illuminates an essential spiritual truth.

In hiddenness, in the most silent of sufferings, diamonds are created.

The second interesting thing about diamonds is that without the unprecedented pressure they experience, they would stagnate and remain as mundane carbon. But, when pressure comes, it saves the diamond from the death of stagnation. This helps us grasp a fundamental principle of spiritual growth: no pressure, no development. While it is true that some people abandon faith during times of pressure, it is rare to find a hero of the faith who has not experienced great pressure.

It is in the times of most pressure that I have grown the most spiritually. Many things have happened to me in my life that I would never want to go through again. Yet, I also know that if I hadn't had those things, I would not be the person God has made me today. Those moments of difficulty, pain, and pressure also have been some of the deepest moments of growth. No pressure, no depth.

Diamonds are made pure by intense pressure. We put them on wedding rings to symbolize purity. We have a quality system that measures the purity of the diamond. That purity, like the purity of holiness, is when our character and our hearts and our minds and our thoughts and our actions align themselves with God's actions, heart, and character. In this life, we can only choose to be holy when faced with tests, temptations, and the pressure of compromise. This teaches us that diamonds are made pure by intense pressure. So too are we. No pressure, no holiness.

KEY IDEA: *Spiritual authority, created in moments of pressure, will be the essential leadership quality in our gray zone moment.*

Pressure confers on us authority. An intelligent person can amass academic qualifications. A person with charisma, personality, and ability can amass a following. The natural communicator can capture the attention of a crowd. The gifted administrator and manager can make sure that an organization runs smoothly. All these things can be valuable additions to one's leadership, yet in the kingdom of God, they can never be the bow of the boat that cuts through the choppy seas. Only spiritual authority can cut through in our gray zone moment. The world is overdosing on hype, intelligence, cynicism, and charisma posing as leadership. What the world hungers for is leadership born of spiritual authority.

How is this authority developed? "You can't develop authority in the barracks; you have to get on the front lines,"[17] Rob Reimer tells us. "There is no match for developing authority like being in the battle."[18] Spiritual authority will be the essential leadership quality in our gray zone moment. So it is vital to understand. No pressure, no spiritual authority.

We have been taught by the great strongholds of our day, whether formed with a structure of secularism or cultural Christianity (or a hybrid of both), that pressure is a bad thing. That it is possible to live life and walk through the raindrops without getting wet. So as the cultural pressure increases against the church in our gray zone moment and we find ourselves in a wilderness, those who turn to God, who choose not to run from the wilderness, who seek His presence in the wilderness, will be transformed with spiritual authority.

RECAP: THREE KEY TAKEAWAYS

- The presence of God turns the hard ground into holy ground.

- In the wilderness, David learned that God was his ultimately stronghold.

- Spiritual authority, created in moments of pressure, is the crucial leadership quality in our gray zone moment.

Conclusion

Flight MH129 Kuala Lumpur to Melbourne, February 2020

I am flying over the Java Sea, not far from the Sunda Strait and the island of Krakatoa. The cabin is sparsely filled. The passengers who haven't canceled their flights because of the pandemic are wearing masks, which will soon become a regular part of life worldwide. In the quiet of the hum of the engines, I am hit by the sense that everything is going to change.

For the last few days, I have been in Kuala Lumpur, Malaysia, speaking at a conference with leaders from all over the region. I am immediately struck by the difference in approach to the pandemic between many Asian Christian leaders I speak to and my pastor friends in the West. Many pastors and leaders in the West seem barely aware of what is happening in Wuhan and have little thought that it may soon impact the environment in which they lead. Their minds are invested in the projects and plans they already have on the calendar, with barely a thought that what was happening in Wuhan could upend their world. In contrast, many of the Asian pastors are already preparing for the impact of the pandemic.

To my surprise, I learn that some leaders at the conference are already preparing for the possibility that they may have to run their services digitally as the pandemic prevents in-person worship. How am I going to transition my church entirely online? This was a possibility I had never pondered or prepared for.

I think back to a meeting I had only a few months earlier with a ministry reaching out to Persians across the world. Across Melbourne, like many places around the world, a steady stream of Persian people have been turning up in churches, many giving their lives to Jesus in what is a modern-day revival. What makes this move of God more remarkable is that the Persians have been an unreached people group for millennia. Yet more Persians have come to faith in Jesus in the last twenty years than in the previous thirteen centuries.[1] In this meeting, I learned of the way that Persians, unable to worship freely in their native Iran, instead are being reached for Jesus and discipled through online services. At the meeting in 2019, I was shown a video where a small group of Persian Christian musicians in London worship in their native tongue, Farsi. This recording is then downloaded by believers in Iran, and throughout the Persian diaspora, across the world.

Thousands of Persians cannot worship freely in person; they can only meet through online worship. Yet the Persian church is exponentially growing. The dynamics that we have explored in this book are borne out in the Persian revival. The events of the Iranian revolution in 1979 threw millions of Persians into a gray zone. The revolution radically transformed the society in which they lived. Many left their homeland and were scattered across the world. The Iranian authorities have actively attempted to suppress the church in Iran, imprisoning believers. The move of God that has occurred among Persians has taken place in a wilderness. And in that wilderness, they have met the presence of God. The seeds of renewal that

God had sowed in Persian hearts had lain dormant yet germinated in the extreme soil that emerged after 1979.

Describing how the church in Iran has grown, Mark Bradley writes in his inspiring book *Too Many to Jail*, "Wanting to eliminate Persian-speaking Christianity from Iran, the government from the mid-1980s put more and more pressure on the official churches to exclude Iranians from a Muslim background. Their campaign has been largely successful."[2] However, through their education in the wilderness, the church in Iran has discovered the hidden source of kingdom power, the power laws that confound the wise. Bradley continues, "There are very few public Christian meetings in Iran in Persian. But this success is a Pyrrhic victory. For out of this persecution against the official churches, the house churches have been born." The hard ground with God for the Persian church has become holy ground. "Many have suffered. But the result is that now there are more purified Christians in Iran who are passionate to spread the Gospel of Jesus."[3] The wilderness is the furnace of transformation. It's where we encounter the presence.

As church went online at the start of the pandemic, our church, like many, struggled. People left. Some deconstructed their faith. Others had to leave as our city entered one of the longest and strictest lockdowns in the world. Then, one night, I found myself again looking up that online Persian worship that I had seen at that meeting in the months before the pandemic hit. As I listened, I couldn't understand the words, but I realized something. The Persian church had been ahead of us the whole time.

The Persians had been working with the limitation of online church long before the pandemic hit. What so many in the West saw as the limitations of not being able to meet in person was, for the Persian church, not only a limitation but also a leverage point that God had used to grow the church in Iran and in the diaspora across the world.

As we move into the gray zone, it is the weak to whom the eyes of the Western church must look to learn.

THE SEA NOW PLAYS

It is the final day of writing this book. Ready to work, I have made myself a coffee and checked the news on my phone. The newspaper has a story about Krakatoa. It is a reprint of the newspaper's report of the explosion, telegraphed to their correspondent, precisely 138 years ago. I marvel at the coincidence of finishing this book on the same date that the news of Krakatoa's eruption reached Australia. I sit and read the contemporary account of the explosion.

After giving an account of the devastation that the volcano had wrought, the correspondent to the *Sydney Morning Herald* ends his dispatch with the evocative line: "Where Mount Krakatoa stood the sea now plays."[4]

The correspondent feverishly telegraphing his account back to Australia could never have known that Krakatoa would rise again. He could never have imagined that where burnt earth smoldered, a vast canvas of life would reappear. He could know nothing of the seeds, lying dormant, that would germinate and grow into mighty trees. At that moment, all he could see was destruction.

Maybe this is what you see now as you look out upon the world. The places you lead, your church, perhaps even your life. Where your dreams and vision and hope stood like mountains, now only the sea plays. But don't forget the sea plays because the Spirit hovers above it, for the moment where there is only sea and formless earth is precisely the moment before creation.

Acknowledgments

Thanks: To the team at Moody for their hard work. This book was written during the 2021 pandemic lockdown in Melbourne. So an extra big thanks to Trudi for your support, and to my children Grace, Hudson, and Billy. Thanks to David for writing the foreword and for alerting me to the digestive abilities of the cassowary. Also, lots of thanks to the Red Church team.

Notes

CHAPTER 1: THE END OF AN ERA

1. Randall L. Schweller, *Maxwell's Demon and the Golden Apple: Global Discord in the New Millennium* (Baltimore: John Hopkins University Press, 2014), 1.

2. John Micklethwait and Adrian Wooldridge, *The Wake Up Call: Why the Pandemic Has Exposed the Weakness of the West—and How to Fix It* (London: Short Books, 2020), 19.

3. Peter Gay, *Weimar Culture: The Outsider as Insider* (New York: W. W. Norton, 1968), 2.

4. James Meeks, "In 1348," *London Review of Books*, April 2, 2020, https://www.lrb.co.uk/the-paper/v42/n07/james-meek/in-1348.

5. Dani Rodrik, "Will COVID-19 Remake the World?," Project Syndicate, April 6 2020, https://www.project-syndicate.org/commentary/will-covid19-remake-the-world-by-dani-rodrik-2020-04.

6. Richard Dobb, James Manyika, and Jonathan Woetzel, *No Ordinary Disruption: The Four Global Forces Breaking All the Trends* (New York: Public Affairs, 2015), 314.

7. Adam Tooze, *Shutdown: How Covid Shook the World's Economy* (London: Allen Lane, 2021), 292.

8. Tooze, *Shutdown*, 293.

9. See Arundhati Roy, "The Pandemic Is a Portal," *Financial Times*, April 3, 2020, https://www.ft.com/content/10d8f5e8-74eb-11ea-95fe-fcd274e920ca.

10. Tyler Cowen, "Science Fiction Is Coming to Life All around Us," Bloomberg, May 18, 2021, https://www.bloomberg.com/opinion/articles/2021-05-17/science-fiction-is-coming-to-life-all-around-us.

CHAPTER 2: REBIRTH

1. Simon Winchester, *Krakatoa: The Day the World Exploded: August 27, 1883* (London: Penguin, 2003), 465.

CHAPTER 3: THE VICTORIAN INTERNET

1. Ben Wilson, *Heyday: The 1850s and the Dawn of the Global Age* (London: Weidenfeld & Nicholson, 2016), 411.

2. Simon Winchester, *Krakatoa: The Day the World Exploded: August 27, 1883* (London: Penguin, 2003), 236.

3. Quoted in Tom Standage, *The Victorian Internet: The Remarkable Story of the Telegraph and the Nineteenth Century's On-line Pioneers* (New York: Walker & Company, 1998), 158.

4. Winchester, *Krakatoa*, 183.

5. See Marshall McLuhan and Bruce R. Powers, *The Global Village: Transformations in World Life and Media in the 21st Century* (Oxford: Oxford University Press, 1989), 98.

6. See chapter 1 of Fredrick H. White, *Degeneration, Decadence and Disease in the Russian* Fin de Siècle: *Neurasthenia in the Life and Work of Leonid Andreev* (Manchester, UK: Manchester University Press, 2014).

7. Greg Daugherty, "The Brief History of 'Americanitis,'" *Smithsonian*, March 25, 2015, https://www.smithsonianmag.com/history/brief-history-americanitis-180954739/.

8. See chapter 1 of Stefan Zweig, *The World of Yesterday: Memoirs of a European* (London: Pushkin Press, 2009).

9. See John Charles Pollock with Ian Randall, *The Keswick Story: The Authorized History of the Keswick Convention—Updated!* (Fort Washington, PA: CLC, 2006).

10. D. Martyn Lloyd-Jones, *From Fear to Faith: Rejoicing in the Lord in Turbulent Times* (Nottingham UK: IVP, 1997), 20–21.

11. Pollock with Randall, *The Keswick Story*, 15.

12. David W. Bebbington, *The Dominance of Evangelicalism: The Age of Spurgeon and Moody* (Leicester, UK: IVP, 2005), 101.

13. Edwin H. Friedman, *A Failure of Nerve: Leadership in the Age of the Quick Fix* (New York: Church Publishing, 1999), 59.

14. Friedman, *A Failure of Nerve*, 63.

15. Pollock with Randall, *The Keswick Story*, 19.

CHAPTER 4: LIFE AND LEADERSHIP ON SECULAR AUTOPILOT

1. Adolf Berle, quoted in Stephen Wertheim, *Tomorrow, the World: The Birth of U.S. Global Supremacy* (Cambridge, MA: Belknap Press, 2020), 47.

2. Isaiah Bowman, quoted in Laurence H. Shoup and William Minter, *Imperial Brain Trust: The Council on Foreign Relations and United States Foreign Policy* (New York: Monthly Review Press, 1977), 163.

3. Wertheim, *Tomorrow, the World*, 7.

4. Ayesha Ramachandran, *The World Makers: Global Imagining in Early Modern Europe* (Chicago: University of Chicago Press, 2015), 14.

5. Walter Lippmann, quoted in David Milne, *Worldmaking: The Art and Science of American Diplomacy* (New York: Farrar, Strauss, and Giroux, 2015), 309–10.

CHAPTER 5: THE AMERICAN CENTURY

1. Alexei Yurchak, *Everything Was Forever, Until It Was No More: The Last Soviet Generation* (Princeton, NJ: Princeton University Press, 2005), 16.

2. Barbara W. Tuchman, *A Distant Mirror: The Calamitous 14th Century* (Harmondsworth, UK: Penguin, 1979), xxi–xxii.

CHAPTER 6: BIRTH OF A NETWORKED AGE

1. Stefan J. Link, *Forging Global Fordism: Nazi Germany, Soviet Russia, and the Contest over the Industrial Order* (Princeton, NJ: Princeton University Press, 2020), 4.

2. Link, *Forging Global Fordism*, 5.

3. Lyndon Baines Johnson, quoted in Roger D. Launius, "Sputnik and the Origins of the Space Age," NASA History Division, https://history.nasa.gov/sputnik/sputorig.html.

4. Alex Abella, *Soldiers of Reason: The RAND Corporation and the Rise of the American Empire* (Boston: Mariner Books, 2008), 141–42.

5. Yuval Levin, *The Fractured Republic: Renewing America's Social Contract in the Age of Individualism* (New York: Basic Books, 2016), 46.

6. Thomas Hylland Eriksen, *Globalization: The Key Concepts* (New York: Routledge, 2020), 7.

7. Henry Kissinger, *World Order: Reflections on the Character of Nations and the Course of History* (London: Penguin, 2015), 344–45.

8. Adam Segal, *The Hacked World Order: How Nations Fight, Trade, Maneuver, and Manipulate in the Digital Age* (New York: Public Affairs, 2016), 33.

9. Joshua Cooper Ramo, *The Seventh Sense: Power, Fortune and Survival in the Age of Networks* (New York: Little, Brown and Company, 2016), 57.

10. See Paul Kennedy, *The Rise and Fall of the Great Powers: Economic Change and Military Conflict from 1500 to 2000* (New York: Random House, 1987).

11. See Yan Xuetong, *Leadership and the Rise of the Great Powers* (Princeton, NJ: Princeton University Press, 2019).

12. For a recent and popular version of this theory, see Graham Allison, *Destined for War: Can America and China Escape Thucydides's Trap?* (Boston: Houghton Mifflin Harcourt, 2017).

13. Peter Frankopan, *The Silk Roads: A New History of the World* (London: Bloomsbury, 2015), xvi.

14. Katherine, "Why Is French Considered the Language of Diplomacy?," Legal Language Services, December 7, 2016, https://www.legallanguage.com/legal-articles/language-of-diplomacy/.

15. See Malcolm Gladwell, *The Tipping Point: How Little Things Can Make a Big Difference* (London: Abacus, 2000).

16. Bjorn Thomassen, *Liminality and the Modern: Living Through the In-Between* (Farnham, UK: Ashgate, 2017), 1.

17. Niall Ferguson, *The Square and the Tower: Networks, Hierarchies and the Struggle for Global Power* (London: Allen Lane, 2017), xxv.

18. Alister E. McGrath, *Christianity's Dangerous Idea: The Protestant Revolution—A History from the Sixteenth Century to the Twenty-First* (New York: HarperOne, 2007), 24–25.

19. John Robb, *Brave New War: The Next Stage of Terrorism and the End of Globalization* (Hoboken, NJ: Wiley, 2007), 95.

20. Manuel Castells, *The Rise of the Network Society*, The Information Age: Economy, Society and Culture, vol. 1 (Oxford: Blackwell, 1996), 3.

21. See David Goodhart, *The Road to Somewhere: The Populist Revolt and the Future of Politics* (London: Hurst & Company, 2017).

22. Stephen D. King, *Grave New World: The End of Globalization, the Return of History* (New Haven, CT: Yale University Press, 2017), 7.

23. Jeremy Rifkin, *The Age of Access: How the Shift from Ownership to Access Is Transforming Modern Life* (London: Penguin, 2000), 259.

24. Fareed Zakaria, *The Post-American World* (New York: Allen Lane, 2008), 4–5.

25. Charles A. Kupchan, *No One's World: The West, The Rising Rest, and the Coming Global Turn* (Oxford: Oxford University Press, 2012), 5.

CHAPTER 7: A NON-ANXIOUS PRESENCE IN AN ANXIOUS AGE

1. Patrick O'Neil, "Brunswick's Good Karma Network Shuts amid Claims of 'Toxic Positivity,' Racism," *The Age*, August 21, 2021, https://www.theage.com.au/national/victoria/brunswick-s-good-karma-network-shuts-amid-claims-of-toxic-positivity-racism-20210821-p58kq4.html.

2. David Kinnaman and Mark Matlock, *Faith for Exiles: 5 Ways for a New Generation to Follow Jesus in Digital Babylon* (Grand Rapids: Baker, 2019), 25.

3. Kinnaman and Matlock, *Faith for Exiles*, 27.

4. Edwin H. Friedman, *A Failure of Nerve: Leadership in the Age of the Quick Fix* (New York: Church Publishing, 1999), 65.

5. Friedman, *A Failure of Nerve*, 74.

6. Friedman, *A Failure of Nerve*, 74.

7. Friedman, *A Failure of Nerve*, 70.

8. Friedman, *A Failure of Nerve*, 245.

CHAPTER 8: FROM GRAY ZONE TO COMFORT ZONE

1. For more on how castles emerged from the decline of the Roman Empire, see Tom Holland, *Millennium: The End of the World and the Forging of Christendom* (London: Little, Brown, 2008), 140–41.

2. Lewis Mumford, *The City in History: Its Origins, Its Transformations, and Its Prospects* (London: Secker & Warburg, 1961), 15.

3. Ronald F. Ingelhart, *Cultural Evolution: People's Motivations are Changing, and Reshaping the World* (Cambridge, UK, 2018), 8.

4. John H. Walton, *The Lost World of Adam and Eve: Genesis 2–3 and the Human Origins Debate* (Downers Grove, IL: IVP, 2015), 48.

5. Dan P. McAdams, *The Redemptive Self: Stories American Live By* (Oxford: Oxford University Press, 2013), 271.

CHAPTER 9: LEADING FROM THE COMFORT ZONE

1. See Judith M. Bardwick, *Danger in the Comfort Zone: From Boardroom to Mailroom—How to Break the Entitlement Habit That's Killing American Business* (New York: AMACOM, 1995).

2. Edwin H. Friedman, *A Failure of Nerve: Leadership in the Age of the Quick Fix* (New York: Church Publishing, 1999), 67.

3. See Zeynep Tufekci, *Twitter and Tear Gas: The Power and Fragility of Networked Protest* (New Haven, CT: Yale University Press, 2017).

4. See Bruno Macaes, *History Has Begun: The Birth of a New America* (London: Hurst & Company, 2020).

5. Phillip K. Dick, quoted in Brooke Gladstone, *The Trouble with Reality: A Rumination on Moral Panic in Our Time* (New York: Workman Publishing, 2017), 4–5.

6. Kurt Andersen, *Fantasyland: How America Went Haywire: A 500-Year History* (New York: Ebury Press, 2017), 429.

7. First Samuel 13:14.

8. Brigit Katz, "Scientists Grew Palm Trees from 2,000-Year-Old Seeds," *Smithsonian*, February 7, 2020, https://www.smithsonianmag.com/ smart-news/scientists-grew-palm-trees-2000-year-old-seeds- 180974164/.

9. Simon Winchester, *Krakatoa: The Day the World Exploded: August 27, 1883* (London: Penguin, 2003), 465.

10. Bruce L. Webber and Ian E. Woodrow, "Cassowary Frugivory, Seed Defleshing and Fruit Fly Infestation Influence the Transition from Seed to Seedling in the Rare Australian Rainforest Tree, Ryparosa Sp. Nov. 1 (Achariaceae)," *Functional Plant Biology* 31, no. 5 (2004): 505–16, doi.org/10.1071/FP03214.

11. Rob Reimer, *Pathways to the King: Living a Life of Spiritual Renewal and Power* (Franklin, TN: Carpenter's Son Publishing, 2013), 150.

CHAPTER 10: FROM EFFICIENCY TO ADAPTATION

1. Stanley McChrystal with Tantum Collins, David Silverman, and Chris Fussell, *Team of Teams: New Rules of Engagement for a Complex World* (London: Penguin, 2015), 2.

2. Ted G. Lewis, *Book of Extremes: Why the 21st Century Isn't Like the 20th Century* (New York: Springer, 2014), v.

3. Margaret Heffernan, *Uncharted: How to Navigate the Future Together* (New York: Avid Reader Press, 2020), xii.

4. Heffernan, *Uncharted*, xii–xiii.

5. Steven H. Strogatz, *Nonlinear Dynamics and Chaos: With Applications to Physics, Biology, Chemistry, and Engineering* (Boca Raton, FL: CRC Press, 2015), 8–9.

6. Stanley McChrystal with Tantum Collins, David Silverman, and Chris Fussell, *Team of Teams: New Rules of Engagement for a Complex World* (London: Penguin, 2015), 2–3.

7. Stephen P. Waring, *Taylorism Transformed: Scientific Management Theory since 1945* (Chapel Hill, NC: University of North Carolina Press, 1991), 40.

8. Robert J. Schiller, *Narrative Economics: How Stories Go Viral and Drive Major Events* (Princeton, NJ: Princeton University Press, 2019), 49, 57.

9. John Authers, "Don't Call Bitcoin a Bubble. It's an Epidemic.," Bloomberg, June 8, 2021, https://www.bloomberg.com/opinion/articles/2021-06-09/don-t-call-bitcoin-a-bubble-it-s-an-epidemic?srnd=opinion.

10. Ricard Sole and Santiago F. Elena, *Viruses as Complex Adaptive Systems* (Princeton, NJ: Princeton University Press, 2019), x.

11. See McChrystal with Collins, Silverman, and Fussell, *Team of Teams*.

12. David Kilcullen, *The Dragons and the Snakes: How the Rest Learned to Fight the West* (Oxford: Oxford University Press, 2020).

13. Alan has shared this in various forums, though I first heard this from him in conversation.

14. Kilcullen, *The Dragons and the Snakes*, 40.

15. Dan Pronk, Ben Pron, Tim Curtis, "Need Lessons in Resilience? Take Notes from This Book by Aussie SAS Veterans," *The Age*, August 8, 2021, https://www.theage.com.au/culture/books/lessons-in-resilience-from-the-battlefield-20210726-p58d4d.html.

CHAPTER 11: THE ANXIOUS FRONTIER

1. Richard Slotkin, *The Fatal Environment: The Myth of the Frontier in the Age of Industrialization, 1800–1890* (Norman, OK: Oklahoma University Press, 1985), 11.

2. Jerry Rubin, quoted in Christopher Lasch, *The Culture of Narcissism: American Life in the Age of Diminishing Expectations* (London: Abacus, 1980), 15.

3. Timothy Melley, *Empire of Conspiracy: The Culture of Paranoia in Postwar America* (Ithaca, NY: Cornell University Press, 2000), vii.

4. Hugh Brogan, *The Penguin History of the USA* (London: Penguin, 1999), 220.

5. Gilbert Murray, *Five Stages of Greek Religion* (Mineola, NY: Dover Publishing, 2002), 130.

6. Rosalind Murray, quoted in Thomas Bertonneau, "Rosalind Murray on Barbarization," VoegelinView, January 27, 2020, https://voegelinview.com/rosalind-murray-on-barbarization/.

7. Donald G. Mostrom, *Intimacy with God* (Wheaton, IL: Tyndale, 1983), 16.

8. Mostrom, *Intimacy with God*, 16.

9. Mostrom, *Intimacy with God*, 18–19.

10. Mostrom, *Intimacy with God*, 19–20.

CHAPTER 12: GAINING A HEAVENLY ORIENTATION

1. Robert Coram, *Boyd: The Fighter Pilot Who Changed the Art of War* (New York: Back Bay Books, 2002), 335.

2. Coram, *Boyd*, 336.

3. Coram, *Boyd*, 326.

4. See Julia Galef, *The Scout Mindset: Why Some People See Things Clearly and Others Don't* (New York: Penguin, 2021).

5. Dag Hammarskjöld, *Markings* (New York: Ballantine Books, 1983), 152.

6. Meredith G. Kline, *Kingdom Prologue: Genesis Foundations for a Covenantal Worldview* (Eugene, OR: Wipf and Stock, 2006), 31.

7. Kline, *Kingdom Prologue*, 32.

8. James B. Jordan, *Through New Eyes: Developing a Biblical View of the World* (Brentwood, TN: Wolgemuth & Hyatt, 1988), 47.

9. Jordan, *Through New Eyes*, 45.

10. Jordan, *Through New Eyes*, 42.

CHAPTER 13: HIDDEN KINGDOM POWER LAWS

1. First Samuel 17:34–35.

2. Richard Rumelt, *Good Strategy/Bad Strategy: The Difference and Why It Matters* (London: Profile Books, 2011), 22.

3. Rumelt, *Good Strategy/Bad Strategy*, 23.

CHAPTER 14: PRESSURE AND THE PRESENCE

1. Alan Redpath, *The Making of a Man of God: Lessons from the Life of David* (Grand Rapids: Revell, 1962), 17.

2. Redpath, *The Making of a Man of God*, 18.

3. Henri J. M. Nouwen, *The Way of the Heart* (New York: Ballantine, 1981), 9.

4. Nouwen, *The Way of the Heart*, 10.

5. Nouwen, *The Way of the Heart*, 10–11.

6. Nouwen, *The Way of the Heart*, 13–14.

7. Nouwen, *The Way of the Heart*, 14.

8. Corey Russell, *Ancient Paths: Rediscovering Delight in the Word of God* (Shippensburg, PA: Destiny Image, 2012), 132.

9. Phillip Keller, *The Shepherd Trilogy* (Grand Rapids: Zondervan, 1970), 22.

10. Keller, *The Shepherd Trilogy*, 29.

11. Keller, *The Shepherd Trilogy*, 29.

12. Keller, *The Shepherd Trilogy*, 31.

13. Keller, *The Shepherd Trilogy*, 29.

14. John R. O'Neil, *The Paradox of Success: When Winning at Work Means Losing at Life* (New York: Penguin, 1993), 26.

15. R. T. Kendall, *The Anointing: Yesterday, Today, Tomorrow* (London: Hodder & Stoughton, 1998), 146.

16. Kendall, *The Anointing*, 147.

17. Rob Reimer, *Spiritual Authority: Partnering with God to Release the Kingdom* (Franklin, TN: Carpenter's Son, 2020), 218.

18. Reimer, *Spiritual Authority*, 217.

CONCLUSION

1. Lindy Lowry, "Mass Conversions 'Are Happening Right under Our Eyes'—Iran Official Admits," Open Doors USA, August 10, 2019, https://www.opendoorsusa.org/christian-persecution/stories/iran-mass-conversions/.

2. Mark Bradley, *Too Many to Jail: The Story of Iran's New Christians* (Oxford: Monarch, 2014), 203.

3. Bradley, *Too Many to Jail*, 203.

4. "The Volcanic Eruptions in the Straits of Sunda," *Sydney Morning Herald*, September 27, 1883, https://www.smh.com.au/world/asia/flashback-the-deadly-1883-eruption-of-krakatoa-20181224-p50o28.html.

FOR SUCH A TIME AS THIS!

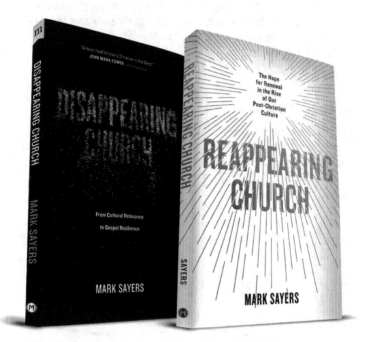

978-0-8024-1335-2   978-0-8024-1913-2

In **Disappearing Church**, Mark Sayers provides the diagnosis for what ails the Church in the post-Christian west. The spirit of this age champions religion without God, Christianity without Christ, and community without commitment. But there is hope. God's call for us to be salt and light in the world begins with renewal and a move of God. In **Reappearing Church**, Mark gives us the treatment for the disease and points us to our hope for the future.

also available as an eBook

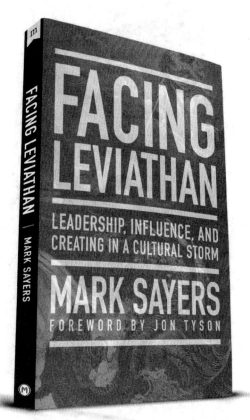